Travelling West

Travelling West

*For Fidelme
with warmest wishes
Rita Kelly
2000*

Rita Kelly

Arlen House
Galway

First printing, September 2000

Published by:

Arlen House
PO Box 222
Galway
Ireland

and

42 Grange Abbey Road
Baldoyle
Dublin 13

ISBN   1-903631-02-5, paperback
        1-903631-03-3, hardback
        1-903631-04-1, limited edition hardback

www.arlenhouse.ie

Cover design based on a painting by Pauline Bewick
Design work: Dunleavy Design, Galway
Typesetting: Arlen House
Printed by: ColourBooks, Baldoyle, Dublin 13

for Edel Connolly

Acknowledgements

The author would like to register her thanks to:-

Muireann Ní Chonaill
Arts Officer, Laois County Council

Catriona O'Reilly
Arts Officer, Cavan County Council

Jane Meally
Education Unit, Portlaoise Prison

for whom she worked on various projects and residencies during the preparation of this collection.

She would also like to acknowledge The Arts Council/An Chomhairle Ealaíon as co-funders of the Writer-in-Residence scheme, and co-funders, with the Department of Justice and Law Reform, of the Writers-in-Prison scheme. She is also grateful to Poetry Ireland and its Writers-in-Schools programme. She thanks the Irish Writers' Centre for the co-funding of Workshops with various Writers' Groups.

Some of the poems have been published, sometimes in altered versions, in the following outlets:

Books Ireland; Cavan Anthology 2000; Comhar; Departures New Series; Poetry Now 2000; Laois Anthology 1999; Munster Literature Centre Newsletter; Or Volge L'Anno, Dedalus Dublin 1998; *Poetry Ireland Review; Pros and Cons*, Portlaoise Prison; *Southward*.

Contents

What if

Hills and hedges are confining things,
what if looking beyond
there are no vast spaces to fill with doubt
and desperation
no far horizon, no unfathomable quietness.
What if measured days and nights
and twilights and seasons of slight change
and sweet moments of shared silence
when a page rustles in the lamplight.
What if you and I
unified on a tempestuous sea
manage to withstand the immensity
steering clear of the heart's fear and the lure
of losing all, of losing everything in some
tossed twist and turn of an outrageous
infinity.

The Irish Lesson

'There is one use amongst them, to keepe their cattle and to live
themselves the most part of the yeare in boolies, pasturing upon
the mountaine, and the waste wilde places'.

Spenser, *View of the State of Ireland*

'In summer time they drive their cattle to the mountaines,
where such as looke to the cattle live in small cabbins for that
season'.

O'Flaherty, *Iar-Connaught*

A young girl comes down from the hills of Bilbo
to a convent school in the plains, no longer run
by celibates. They mock the place from where she comes,
Bil-bo, Bil-bo, as if it should have a new and polished
Guggenheim facing down a Cantabrian sea. Bilbao is too
the *buaile bó*, the milking-place in summer pasturage,
calm and soft and sweet places of nurture. Places where
los vaqueros trusted their cows to carry their infants
on their horns. And when *los vaqueros* came down to the
towns of the plains to worship,
there was a door just for them
in the church, and they knelt and sat apart from
the rich and the respected.

This young girl knows exactly what a harmonium is –
she has heard it wheeze on damp Sundays,
pumped through the paces of a communion service.
She is a Protestant in an unlikely place, Anglican,
well watered down in the sodden reaches of regurgitated
grass. Who knows?
Perhaps the gilt-edged invitations in cursive script
reach to this remote place of no happenings,
telling of Lambeth,
bishops and conferences and tea
on the lawn of the Palace.
But there is no Dean here, no Archdeacon, no precinct of
privilege, just breathtaking views of distance
and the distinct possibility of multiple narrations.

Why a convent school? By now well deplete of virgins
and all their mischief. The Protestant ethos is
unchallenged
and safe with these latter-day nuns.
It is an affiliation of choice.
No far-removed boarding places of individual
desperations and whimperings in the night
for loss of place and local cadence.
No, this girl knows what a harmonium is, and very likely
knows a harmony too
in the round and revolution of her resplendent mornings.
Her name is Spenser, though there are no echoes
of Colin Clouts come home again … flow gently, flow
and it has flown through the ages
of bright opportunity and dark dispossession.

You, my dear daughter of the Spensers, have kept
the *buaile bó* intact, you have faced the ferocious winds
and won your footing,
your people sleep safe in the arms of Jesus,

and you have planted trees, oak and beech,
strong and deep-rooted.
Settling kind of trees, creating a canopy
for our common prayer.
Oaks are slow and very slow, stretching all our resources
of patience to the very rim of the future.

I teach you Irish, another way of wondering at the world,
you are no Faërie Queen or indeed am I,
yet that other Queen's copybooks are not unlike your
own.
It is as if the royal hand had traced the new alphabet but
yesterday.
Trying to go beyond the lines of anger and hatred,
trying to glimpse horizons of justice.
Who taught her, Elizabeth 1, her Irish? Shane O'Neill?
That pompous ass. Who cares.
She shed her circumstance for the inclusive thing.

Lambeths and Lambegs, part of the peripherals,
as we reach down into the imprisoned voice of
Caitlín Maude,*
crying out of some choking reality,
some claustrophobic hell.
We tread carefully, releasing her words,
restoring her voice.
A different voice from a far-distant place,
which will this evening resonate
up in those fair places and pastures new of green comfort
and refuge for weary cows
lifting themselves up out of the depastured dusk
of the flat plains and the ordinary.

*Caitlín Maude (1941–1982). Irish poet, singer, dramatist.
Born Ros Muc, Conamara, Co Galway.

The Visibility of Difference

for Kay Wilde, with affection

'Identity is as slippery as a fish', Elizabeth Bowen

There is no use in pretending
we're not different –
your hair is different
even before we take a rib
from each and peer at it
under a high-powered microscope.
We might both be categorised
as white, Caucasian, female;
well, if we committed a felony
or indeed if we were found dead
in suspicious circumstances,
or if there was a tag tied to our toe
in some freezing cabinet
waiting to be poked
by some pathologist.

But I can't feel safe in the arms of Jesus,
it is foreign to me,
just as is the colour, the flags
the tablets of stone remembrance,
even the tea.
And yet I have come and sought you out
in the Close and shadow of this Cathedral,
to talk about the town we have both left,
you in 1939 and I in 1972.
How we love to name the names,
to recall the places and to savour their flavour,
the lie and turn of a hedgerow or a well-lit street,
to meet and see again the faces
of those so familiar day after day –
and now we call them up out of the nooks and crevices
of memory.

We skirt each other a little,
make the allowance
the passage of time, the side you lived,
not a syllable of your accent has changed
it is as homely and as wholesome
as this apple tart you have baked.
You could be my mother-in-law,
God, whatever that is, a very warm woman
whom I loved dearly and deeply
as she laughed at the fact that she had
hit a bold girl with a slate
- they were real slates then –
for calling her and her little sisters 'Jumpers'
in the midday melee of the nuns' schoolyard.
My mother-in-law was Maud Sproule
and her sisters were Isabella and Belinda
how these names must have rung against
the towering walls of the convent.
Later the little sisters left for Manitoba

and became Protestants again in the long
reaches of personal and private choice
after the spirited defence ...
And Maud would mother a youth fired
with a dark and destructive instinct
to creep along the border with gelignite
driven by some vision strong enough
to kill and be killed for –
and his cousins disappeared, gone under,
gone underground, we still do not know,
all the mothering instinct and lines of energy
cannot say where they are ...
But the 'Bomber' survived, something screwy
with his legs, who came to our town in
the three-wheeled car, bright blue,
a car especially designed for disability
and a pension too, he had driven all the way
from his home in England.

I feared meeting this man.
Harmless could be used of him,
but it would say nothing precise.
He was overweight with a very red face.
Told little stories about fishing,
his family and remembered characters in town,
all their nicknames and escapades.
He had a kind face.
- Useless, Maud said, like his mother, Susie,
like our own Isabella, it runs,
this she could say with such kindness.

I feared that he would smell of nitro-glycerine.
I feared he would smell of seared flesh
and scattered limbs lodged with metallic things.
I did not know the smell of nitro-glycerine,

I would know later that it eased the pain
in my husband's chest, the pain that I too
could feel in my chest and along my arms
when I awoke in the middle of the night
in a bed full of terror.

When I hear your voice as it resounds
in this pleasant kitchen beside the Cathedral Wall
I hear and see and smell our past.
You ask if I remember that nice man
who fitted my shoes, of course I do,
he was such a nice man, talked pleasantries
with my father, or indeed my mother,
across my head as I struggled with
patented leather and prettiness.
- Yes, she has a very high instep.
That was a nice way of saying
that I had a chubby little foot
that needed something broad and sensible
none of this fancy stuff.
I can smell the opened boxes of shoes.
I can hear the ruffle of the thin tissue
paper when the lids came off.
I can still see that man climb the well-polished ladder
to reach higher and higher into the shelves
of neatly packed boxes of shoes
to get that 'something just right for her'.

Later, they said, the nice man
drove North for the 12th
that he wore a bowler hat and a sash.
He marched.

I can hear the gravel crunch beneath the feet of the men
moving slowly out of the Protestant Church,
the Church with the broken bell, Pixie Hobbs whammed
the back of a big iron frying-pan
to call the people of the Glen to prayer.
I can see the gleaming black shoes and boots,
some were tan too and ox-blood red.
My father held my hand in his, gentle yet firm.
I wanted to go into that Church, not stand small
in a huge huddle of neighbours, men mostly,
shifting uneasily on the grass of the graveyard's edge.
My father's cousin was in there with her dead husband,
he had the same name as the man in the shoe-shop,
their house was bright and full of laughter when we
visited.
Yet my father too stands back from the affection
of family, from the need of those in need, obeying
some deep divisive and very stupid law of the narrow
mind.

Suddenly the world is too tight.
It pinches like an ill-fitting shoe.

Now your George is safe in the arms of Jesus.
There is a void in this pleasant kitchen
where he sat.
Of course it's not the same, but you braveface it
and smile to think that you still come breathless through
the door
to tell him ...

As the evening gathers in, we go gently across the Close,
and along the precise paths through the weathered
headstones,

walking and chatting, on into the Cathedral.
The old hesitations are as distant as childhood itself.
There is a cool vast interior shot through
with maculated light.
The pews, the choirs, the tombs, the carved eagle of the
Evangelist.
There is a slight smell of must.
We stand beneath the tablet to George, remembering him.
Suddenly there is the unmistakable smell of fresh
hazelnuts.
A delicate smell.
There were thousands of hazel along the sand-ridges
of the place we know well, the place from whence we
came.
The same hazels which shimmered in the sound
of the big black frying pan exploding through the decades
of dissent.

An Dá Shaol

I ndilchuimhne Cyril Ó Céirín, 1934–1999, file, múinteoir,
ealaíontóir, ceoltóir is cara den scoth. Léadh an dán seo i láthair
Kit agus a clann mac, i Lios Dún Bhearna le linn ócáid ómóis do
Cyril, Meitheamh 2000.

Feicim thú i gcónaí ar scáth is ar chiumhais
na Sionnaine,
maidin mhíoriúilteach ar chlár an tsaoil,
Kit is na leaids fós
ina gcodladh
faoi easnachaí an bháid.
Tusa amuigh roimh ghuth ar ghéag,
ag léamh na spéire,
is ag cur léirscáil an tsaoil i gcaoi dúinn.
Ag glacadh aeir i d'aonar
os cionn na n-uiscí
is Mílic mhánla á síneadh féin sa chúinne caol
agus i gcúngacht talún sin
idir an t-uisce
is caoldoras álainn Chluain Fearta.

Meabhair is Cúige Mumhan
go smior ionat
mar dhún seasta
os cionn sáile is farraige.

Croí is Cúige Chonnacht
go smior ionat fosta
mar dhath na gréine
ag ceoladh féin i sioscadh na ngiolcach.

Ach anois tá Kit is na leaids
ina n-aonar,
léann siadsan an spéir,
is nuair a chasann
an ghaoth amhrán
thar an Lios
thar an Dún
is tríd an Bhearna isteach –
níl siad ina n-aonar a thuilleadh.

Two Worlds

In fond memory of Cyril Ó Céirín, 1934–1999, poet, teacher, artist, musician and very good friend. This poem was read in the presence of Kit and her sons, in Lisdoonvearna during a tribute to Cyril, June 2000.

I still see you in the shadow on the edge
of the Shannon,
miraculous morning on the face of the earth,
Kit and the lads still
asleep
under the ribs of the boat.
You outside before the dawn chorus,
reading the skies,
putting the map of life in order for us.
Taking the air alone
over the waters
gentle Meeleek stretching itself in the tight corner
and in the small fields
between the water
and the beautiful narrow door of Clonfert.

Intelligence and Munster
deep in you
like a mighty fortress
above the sea.

Heart and Connacht
also deep in you
like the colour of the sun
singing itself in the whispering of the reeds.

But now, Kit and the lads
are alone,
they read the sky,
and when the wind
sings a song
over the Ringfort
over the Fortress
and through the Gap -
they are no longer alone.

translated by Edel Connolly

Joey Dunlop

dealaithe óna ghluaisrothar, dealaithe ón domhan, Mí Iúil, 2000.

É sínte ansin i gculaith buí na gréine,
cos thar chaol a choise aige,
amhail is dá mba
sos beag á chaitheamh aige,
ga nó dhó gréine á nglacadh aige
ar bord loinge
i leaba mhairnéalaigh
nó ar chaiteog bheag
cois trá
i lár an tsamhraidh –

ba é an samhraidh é inniu,
samhradh saibhir,
samhradh brothallach an Iúil,
samhradh gruasholasta,
an fharraige, an spéir,
craiceann na gcloch ceansa
soilseach, te:
ba é an samhradh beo é.

Pillíní beaga ar bhoinn a bhróg
speisialta aige,
pillíní geala chun greim a bhreith.
Na cosa neamhurchóideacha
caite inár dtreo,
gan tada ag breith greama anois,
roth ná bróg,
ach an t-íomhá,
an clogad mór ataithe:
gléas frith-ga-ach faoi iomlán gréine, mheasfá,
is Joey ciúin, socair.
Na paramedics ag rith, ach fós feoite ina rith
chuige.
Iad gléasta i nDayglo dearg, de shíor
ag claonadh chuige
ina gcéimeanna stadaithe.

Grianghraf an nuachtáin caite ina ndosaen
i mburla ag an Filling Station.
Téimid thairis isteach
chun íoc as an ndó-ola
a chothaíonn luas fúinn.

Cloisfimid, mar atá cloiste againn
i lár na hoíche,
i gcasadh na maidine,
i gcupáinín teolaí nide:
Plab!
Craobhóigín beag bídeach á bhriseadh.
Snap!
Smeach!
Luasrothar leaid éicínt briste ina dhá leath
agus eisean sínte i ngealán beag gréine
gan míog nó gíog as.
Is geonáinín gaoithe ag líonadh an nóiméid.

An leaid ar aithne ar na daoine atá rite amach
béaloscailte ...
é ar an mbóthar céanna achar beag ó shin
ag cothú luais is pléisiúir dó fhéin
ar a *thricyclig* nua-fhaighte aige is nua-thugtha dó.

Ach i marbhchiúnas na maidine
níl ann ach síleadh beag fola óna chluas.

Joey Dunlop

separated from his motorbike and from the world, July 2000

He stretched there in a sun-yellow suit,
one foot across his ankle,
as if
he were having a little break,
taking a ray or two of sun
on board ship
in a hammock
or on a little mat
on the beach
in the middle of summer –

it was summer today,
lush summer,
hot July summer
summer of bright faces,
the sea, the sky,
the surface of the smooth stones
lit up, hot:
it was really summer.

The little pads on the sole
of his special shoes,
bright little pads to grip.
The unoffending feet
thrown in our direction,
with nothing to grip now,
wheel or shoe,
but the image,
the big, swollen helmet:
a thing for blocking out the full sun, you'd think,
and Joey quiet, at ease.
The paramedics running, but still static in their run
towards him.
Dressed in red Dayglo, still leaning towards him
in their frozen steps.

The newspaper photograph thrown
in a heap at the Filling Station.
We go in by them
to pay for the fuel-oil
that sustains speed beneath us.

We will hear, as we have heard
in the middle of the night,
in the turning of the morning,
in the little cupped, cosy nest:
Bang!
A tiny, sweet little branch being broken.
Snap!
Smack!
Some lad's motorbike broken in two
and he stretched out in the little patch of sunshine
not a stir out of him.
A little sigh of wind filling the moment.
The lad known to those who run out

open-mouthed ...
he on the same road a little while ago
building speed and pleasure for himself
on his new tricycle.

But in the dead quiet of morning
there's only a little trickle of blood from his ear.

translated by Edel Connolly

Traein na Tulaí Móire

Ní bhíonn fhios againn
cá dtitfidh an scéal
nó cén cúinne den domhan
ina mbeimid nuair a bhrisfidh
an nóiméad.

Bhí mé féin i nDún Éidean, ó thuaidh, i gcéin,
plódaithe le héigse is fuisce is olagón na bpíob
i bpríomhchathair na nOchtú hAoise Déag,
Boswell agus criticí na n-irisí liteartha
ina scuaine thaibhsiúil sna cearnóga
ina bhfuil smúit na gcianta ar a n-aghaidheanna.
Ní liom carraig bhuan Dhún Éidean ná ní liom
dreach dúr an Domhnaigh, ná foisceacht na Banríona
i racht goil, i muinín a croí.
Is fada uaim an t-achar, Banríon ag cailliúint a cinn
in aduaineas Londan.

Tháinig an drochscéal ar maidin,
táim anois ar thraein na Tulaí Móire
ag sní isteach is amach idir na heascracha.
Rachaidh an traein amach go Clara –
áit ina raibh m'athairse óg tráth.
Áit is am go mb'fhada uaidh

lomfhuacht an bháis.
Ritheann an traein ar aghaidh agus sonann na
logainmneacha
atá sáite sa chuimhne ar aon dul leis an roth iarainn
á chiorclú féin ar mhíneadas an iarnróid.
Téim siar, siar arís, sa tslí chéanna ina ndeachaigh sé fhéin
siar
chomh minic sin sul má bhí mé fhéin fiú i gcrot na mbeo.
Inniu, tá sé dulta siar is a aghaidh dúnta
i gcrot na marbh.

Tullamore Train

We don't know
where the news will fall
or in what corner of the world
we will be when
the moment will break.

I was in Edinburgh, in the north, far away,
full of poets and whiskey and wailing bagpipes
in the capital city of the Eighteenth Century,
Boswell and literary critics
ghostly lining the squares
where the smuts of the centuries are in their facades.
Neither the solid rock of Edinburgh nor
the closed dourness of Sunday nor the nearness of the
Queen in a fit of crying,
in the trust of her heart belong to me.
It's a long way away from me, a Queen losing her head
in the foreignness of London.

The bad news came this morning,
I'm now on the Tullamore train
weaving its way in and out between the eskers.
The train will go out to Clara –
a place where my father was young once.

A place and time when
the bare cold of death was so far away from him.
The train runs on and the place-names which are sunk
deep in memory sound in the same movement as the iron
wheel turning itself on the well-worn railway.
I go west,
back again along the same way he himself went back
so often before I was even born.
Today, he is gone back, his face closed in death.

translated by Edel Connolly

The Big House

The moon rides high
in a clear sky above Portlaoise.
The sun is a huge burning orb
and spills red unto the windows of Portlaoise.

The Slieve Blooms lose their substance
and are miraged on the outer rim.
The town is burnished and bright
despite the incarceration.

The gantries swing high above this scene
and this condition.
In the fields the cattle graze and glow,
the people prosper having the sun and moon
simultaneously,
it waxes full.

The walls ride high and grey and hard,
hard as hell,
they hem in and overwhelm –
a place which feels itself strange and dangerous
a place of vaulted anger.

You cannot hear the activity of the living
you cannot hear life driving its articulated truck
you cannot see the bright smile of the lads
heading into the snooker hall close to the Coliseum,
or the woman with her cranky little pomeranian.

You cannot smell that oil and salt and sharpness
of the vinegar in its immediacy, as the young fellow
leaves the chipper,
and rushes back to his thin-wheeled tractor,
his hand diving into the fried-hot chips, bringing
bits of pleasure to his mouth, watering …
knowing that he will spray more and more acres of corn
for hours, until bone-weary of the long day, the vistas
and the smell of the herbicide.

There is a grey in the faces of those you can see.
Incarcerated.
It is a grey which is reflected in the heaped, high up
texture of the local limestone, dug out of some
dank and dark hiding place to suppress the day.

We are tired and nervous for no apparent reason
and the air hangs heavy with the lives we have
squandered,
the futures we have fucked up and funnelled into
this narrow place, this hole, this hell, this hindermost
position of all that is stagnant.

Yes, the gantries swing high above the white mansion
they are putting in place, piece by piece.

There is no Mississippi delta here
just one big gleaming Graceland
for all the poor boys
determined to do themselves
out of the uplift of an early summer's evening –

   we are put to bed early
   where the light and its unusual strength
   taunts us at the window.
   Sometimes we cried ourselves into the morning
   and sometimes we just lay there and longed –

Always hung on the dichotomies, the old divisions,
the just and the damned.
The old dualities, the sun and the moon.
The bright and tantalising rise of Hesperus
spans a space between the curved moon and a sun
which might have dropped off a huge orange tree
in Florida or Seville,
colouring this quiet unwatered hinterland.

The just and the damned produce in the one
the idea of the other,
fashion out of the one
the figure of the other.

We make our way through the evening
not knowing what idea stands at the gate
ready to imprison us for our unlawfulness.
We are Socrates, refusing to hand ourselves the hemlock.

We still believe that we can call
a different narrative out of all the possible narratives
open to us in this profound narcotic state.

We hold on by the slimmest of tendrils
to the thin hope that we might appease ourselves and the
world,
and not be carried out in a stream of black cadillacs
to clog the streets of Memphis
with talent.

Portlaoise

for Pat Boran

In front of me there is a Ford Focus,
it shimmers, bright chrome on a blue background.
The road climbs up to the Windy Gap
and spills down the other side into Stradbally.
Focus, Ford, it takes the curves in front of me,
there are no fords in this riverless stretch of Midland,
at least no obvious ones, bloodied by the historic hordes
crossing and recrossing to lay claim upon the future.

Out over The Heath, away out over it,
the far-distant mountains fold into each other,
over on the East, they lie like sated animals,
and they are dusted with an unseasonable snow
because large pockets of low pressure are pulling
harsh winds out of the Arctic reaches
and throwing hailstones in our face.
And causing the magnolia to cringe,
singeing its delicate and tentative bits and tips
of promising exposure.
Ah, but a blackthorn explodes in the hedgerow.
Tough and tight and tense in the hedgerow.

It has a hard black bark, and I can still feel
the shock of the sloe, its bitterness like a burn
on my tongue, when young, at the far end of this Midland
stretch,
this bog, where blackthorns clung close to the eskers
in the long formative periods of taking everything in.

You have talked about the hawthorn, and that is in June,
much taller than the blackthorn, when it blooms
and blushes, pink-complexioned with a profuse amount
of petals.
We know our hawthorn too,
and the cluster of haws hanging
against the dark leaves, red, and we know that fleshy feel
of this fruit under the tooth,
far less astringent than the black sloe bursting like
a bullet of bitterness.

This Ford Focus cannot be overtaken.
It maintains a steady speed on these narrow
Nineteenth Century kind of roads surfaced for the first
time in black tar during our youth.

But there is Japanese cherry in full flush,
not quite of these parts,
a wood soft as butter under the chisel to make aromatic
cigar boxes.
The cherry lets its blossoms slip in the suburbs along the
high retaining wall of the mental hospital.
We all know these Victorian limestone edifices designed
to make us invisible to the world.
But just then that Ford Focus, slows, and stops to join
all the other cars parked at right-angles to the road
across from the cemetery. They sit and wait. In

before the rush, they will have full view of the hearse
crawling up the hill, followed by the pale faces
who have lost so much in that slowed trip to the
cemetery.
They sit in the Ford Focus looking into that tight place of
stones.

All towns are the same and different.
The givens. The definites. Where the graveyard is,
the mental hospital, the bridge, if there is a river,
where doctors live in fine, well-laid out houses.
And where houses are far less detached, in a hollow
maybe, fold into each other in curves and crescents.
They are named after some local hero
whom we don't know anymore: O'Brien or Harris or
Rafter or whatever –
Harris Terrace, O'Brien Drive and the Rafter Roundabout.
Who are those men who haunt our locations?
These terraces and drives are strewn with broken bits of
chariot wheels happily on meagre grass.
Dogs of all description and kids with dirty little faces
launching themselves on vast adventures in the whirr
of the dismembered pram-wheels.

These are our towns and everything in between.
The houses tucked in along the Main Street,
there is inevitably a Dublin Road,
shabby backyards and gardens,
windows which do not match because
they are the track and spoor of all our attempts
to reshape, reach out and extend ourselves.

There are no smouldering ashpits anymore,
we pay the local lad to take our rubbish

in regulated bins, off our hands.
Take it out into the bog
along the Mountmellick road.
We corral it there. And the lad gets up before dawn
to deliver us of our rubbish.

He drives a very fast and capacious car
of gorgeous curves
along the new asphalt which crosses the bog like a dream.
God, the joy of pressing that accelerator to the floor
and burning fossil fuel, tons of it,
in the big maw of a Mercedes;
having sat on the bare boards of an unsprung cart ...
Oh the hell with that!
And the rain across the face
and the long bright sleán.
Unlike Heaney in Derry, we cut turf,
we did not dig turf.
All that latent pent-up energy
silent of an afternoon but for the watery cry
of a gull flung far in across the wild raspberry
and the bronze gleam of the bog myrtle.

Remembering Máirtín Ó Cadhain
Imprisoned at the Curragh 1939–1944

The Curragh cuts in with all its verdure
across the window of this train.
Furze explode in clusters, yellowing the green.
And horses out for an early morning canter
ease up the little inclines,
rising and falling and trotting on.

Máirtín Ó Cadhain knew it well,
but never this.
Or these bright rich rails and pickets
of the enclosure and its discarded starting gate.
The sport of kings.

No real stomach for it,
Ó Cadhain, republican,
not wanting it to be over
no moving on.

His letters out speak of Russian lessons,
and we puny men and women can later sing

of Chekhov in his stories
connecting to the exotic.

Ó Cadhain just felt the cold,
a bitter Siberian cold,
without any of the common good.
No making that mouth.
No breaking him in.

Bádóireacht

Maidin shamhraidh, roimh ghuth ar ghéag,
roimh bhriseadh ar bith ar an mbrionglóid –
cos amach ar adhmad an urláir go faiteach.
Mé mar ghadaí ar fud an tí, ag éalú chun an tsrutha.

Céimeanna beaga bídeacha trí na garraithe.
Drúcht drisiúil, seancharranna néantógacha,
is bábógaí briste.
An ghrian ag smaoineamh air i rosamh na spéire,
ag marcaíocht go ciúin, aclaí
ar chuisle na n-uiscí: an bád.

An eochair faoi cheilt, faoi chloch.
Tommy Coleman, ba leis an bád aerach seo,
bhí deal déanta againn:
cead agam é a úsáid am ar bith roimh a sé ar maidin
in ainneoin is in aineolas mo thuistí,
iad fós sáite i limistéar na súl dúnta.

Amach liom ag rámhaíocht.
An bád á shlíobadh féin
ar airgead na maidine.

Is na braoiníní beaga ag sileadh go soilseach
solasmhar ó bhruasa an mhaide rámha.

Do bhris mé bealach isteach in aghaidh, i ndromchla
is i ndreach na Sionainne
is do bhris mistéir is miotaseolaíocht mhór
na mochmhaidine isteach orm
faoi na Trí hÁirsí Déaga.

Boating

A summer's morning, before daybreak,
before any breaking at all of the dream -
one foot out on the wooden floor, fearful.
I'm like a thief around the house, escaping to the stream.

Small tiny footsteps through the gardens.
Briary dew, wrecked cars, nettles
and broken dolls.
The sun thinking about it in the glow of the sky.
Rocking quietly, agile
on the pulse of the water: the boat.

The key hidden, under a stone.
Tommy Coleman, owned this happy boat,
we had a done deal:
I could use it any time before six in the morning
in spite of and unknown to my parents
they still stuck in the realm of the closed eye.

Out I went rowing.
The boat caressing itself
on the morning silver.

The little drops dripping brightly
clear off the lips of the oar.

I made my way into the face, the crest and the surface
of the Shannon,
the mystery and the huge myth
of early morning seeped into me
under the Thirteen Arches.

                              translated by Edel Connolly

Droichead na Sionnaine

Mám soilse i lár na hiargúltachta,
b'shin an tsibhialtacht dúinne
ón taobh eile den tSionainn
ó réimsí leathan féir is portach -
Rachra, cathair faoi dhraíocht dúinn.

Do shín is do shín sruth na Sionainne
amach is amach ós ár gcomhar
go dtí go raibh
an tSráidbhaile mar líne tithe,
is soilse spréite ar dhroim an domhain.

D'fhan raidhse an tsamhraidh go léir
faoi thoinn, boladh blasta
an *meadowsweet* –
níor bhacamar riamh lena ainm oifigiúil:
'airgead luachra'.

Chualamar slopaireacht shlim na taoide
ar na céimeanna aolchloiche
ar chúl an tí ... *tír álainn trína chéile* ...
bhí céimeanna mar sin ag gach teach
agus bhí gach teach ina bhád

bunoscionn.
David Copperfield muidne go léir is Betsy Trotwood
i bhfad uainn, b'fhéidir.
Nach rabhamar i lár cruinne cosúil le chuile dhuine
ina áit féin.

Bhí an spéir is na réaltaí go léir ar foluain fúinn.
Iad ar fad casta bunoscionn i dtuilte abhann.

Shannonbridge

A fistful of light in the middle of nowhere,
that was civilisation to us
from the other side of the Shannon
from wide stretches of grass and bog -
Shannonbridge, a magical city to us.

The flow of the Shannon stretched and stretched
out and out in front of us
until there was only
the Village, its line of houses,
and lights spread out on the back of the world.

All the fullness of summer stayed
underwater, fruity smell
of *meadowsweet* -
we never bothered with its formal name:
'silver rushes'.

We heard the smooth splash of the flood
on the limestone steps
at the back of the house ... beautiful, untidy country ...
every house had steps like that
and every house was a boat

upside-down.
We were all David Copperfield and Betsy Trotwood
far away from us, perhaps.
Weren't we the centre of the universe like everyone else
in their own place.

The sky and all the stars floated beneath us.
All turned upside-down in the floods.

translated by Edel Connolly

Cups

for Patrick Galvin and Mary Johnson

From the King's Road to Pimlico
up and down they go.
In and out of shabby Notting Hill pubs
keeping up their East End
long before the low-lives and layabouts
joined in the fashionable flow.

The period was vibrant with canned soup,
transistors, mini coopers and mini skirts,
it was all cheese-cloth and Mary Quant,
flats and flea-markets, Mick Jagger or the Hollies
depending how heavy you liked your rock.

How could we know.
How did any girl know whether at Tottenham Court
or stepping over Putney Bridge
that you had shaped their cups,
pulled, stretched and moulded
right around the clock.

Double shifts and time-and-a-half.
The work ethic was chic
and industry took on a whole new meaning.
Millions of moulded white receptacles passing by
in slow motion, on a conveyor belt, there were black too,
pink and a kind of fleshy beige, but that was a separate
section.

Time and Motion was a storm of possibility.
Quality Control, most certainly, had to do with
lift and separate.

Now Mary, when he walks down the Mall
or crosses at the Metropole,
it is not the amount of newly-registered cars
in Cork that sets him figuring,
he isn't reading the sky either
calculating the rain-clouds blowing in from Mizen.
No, he is reading the cups,
not the shape of things to come
rather the shape of things as they are.

He knows all about our fluctuations
our A's and B's and C's, and double D's.
How snug they fit, how real they are,
we are measured at a glance,
the eye being quicker than the hand.
He'll decide with a quite smile
how much work, if any, is needed
on our foundations.

Wheeling into Oliver Plunkett Street
there are more and more to meet
coming from Cash's lopsided with purchases,
where a woman had taken them
into a kind of private sanctum
to measure and recommend
the best fit, the snuggist cup.

The Glass Case

The butcher reaches across the gigots,
he could be my father, a little old, a little tired,
a little hint of pleasantness, trying to give us
always what we want, no fat, no grizzle ...
a woman near me says she'd like four of those
with the little round bone.

The names of the strange shapes
he, and later I, cut out of the animal
like pieces of an abstract puzzle
remain with me everytime I go to buy
a few chops for the dinner.

The butcher reaches across the gigots
for the centre-loins
they are a deep El Greco red.
- Shall I decapitate the quadruped?
Old Wiley said to the poor women who stood
at their doors viewing the rabbit
held aloft and dead.
He had a wooden leg and cycled a fixed-wheel bicycle.
Poor people stewed a rabbit or a sheepshead.
Old Wiley played cricket too,

his wooden leg resounded across the Green,
an extra wicket.

Strange, we inherit the skills and ways
of our fathers, and the people who peopled their world
stray into a foggy day in November
when all the bits and pieces of ourselves
our pasts and our dismembered presents
gleam in the clean glass
of a moment's forgiveness.

Moments

Hieroglyphics here
riot gear, bog-cotton gone
magnolia jail

Dead water
smooth sanded curves
before laburnum

Wild cherry window
architect Evelyn
hand-washed out

Bowed heads heavy
after daffodils
spelling the spring

Air venting in, some sun,
cold street, low pressure,
singed leaf-buds

Curtains part
main act
moon in the window

Cith Caorthineach   17ú Samhain 1999

do Nóirín Ní Riain, ealaíontóir

Dúradar linn inné
go mbeimis in ann
an sinneán soilse sa spéir, an cith dreigíte,
a aimsiú san oíche aréir.

Níos faide ar aghaidh san iarnóin,
dúradar linn nach mbeimis in ann
toisc go raibh droch-aimsir
á leathnú féin ón Atlantach isteach orainn.

An bháisteach, ní nach ionadh,
agus dlúth chlúdach scamallach idir sinn
agus an tarlacan.
Bheadh an cith caorthineach ag tarlú
is ag spleodrú as ár n-amharc.

Ach in Ionad Ealaíon an Bhainc,
i dtithe na seanPhairliminte,

geal sa Ghealchathair, do shiúil tú isteach
is an chaorthine ag drithliú
i bhfionnadh do fhallainge.
Rithim sa ghluaiseacht fút,
is séiseach do chabhail is do choisíocht.
Binn do ghuth is mór do ghlór,
líonfadh do ghuth an spás seo
mar a líonann sé chuile chúinne
i n-aigne agus i gcroí an éisteora.

Do chlaon tú chuig do sheanchara,
i sruth agus i sileadh na cainte
is d'fhág tú póigín bídeach ar a ghualainn,
i dteannas an nóiméid, i gcion na hoíche
cuireann tú feabhas is maise ar a *chakra*.

Dúirt an Díreanach tráth:

    tá an bhean ann atá caoin banúil
    agus intleachtúil le chéile.
    Tá sí cabhrach i dteannta a bheith meabhrach.
    Is tearc an ghin í. Is seoid í.

Sea mhaise, is seoid thú
i seomra ar bith, i gcomhluadar ar bith,
ag glinniúint i bhflaithiúlacht do chroí
agus i bhfial thuisceanach d'ealaíne is d'amhrán.
Go maire tú i stríoca saibhre na spéire s'againne.
Cith ceana, neart tola,
go mbainfí tú an damhán alla as cluasa cháich.

Meteorite Shower   17th November 1999

for Nóirín Ní Riain, artist

Yesterday they said
we would see
the explosion of light,
the meteorite shower, in the sky, last night.

Later in the afternoon,
they told us we wouldn't,
bad weather
was extending in from the Atlantic.

Rain, no surprise,
and a heavy covering of cloud
between us and the spectacle.
The meteorite shower would happen
and explode out of sight.

But, in the Arts Centre of the Bank,
in the old Houses of Parliament,
bright in the Brightcity, you walked in

and the meteor glittering
in your fur coat.
Rhythm in your movement,
melody in your body and your footsteps.
The sweetness and expansion of your voice,
it would fill this space
as it does every corner
of the listener's heart and mind.

You leaned towards your old friend,
in the stream and flow of conversation
you placed a kiss on his shoulder,
in the compression of the moment,
in the affection of night
you cleared his *chakra*.

Ó Direaín once said:

    there is the woman who is all woman
    tender and intellectual.
    She is helpful as well as thoughtful.
    She is a rare form. She is a jewel.

Yes indeed, you are a jewel
in any room, in any company,
shining in the generosity of spirit
in the understanding of your art, your song.
May you live in the rich striations of sky.
Shower of affection, strength of will.
May you open our ears to the full.

translated by Edel Connolly

Eavan Boland in Carlow

So long ago, aeons out of mind,
way back in the mother of all the Muses: Memory,
when you came along the roads
not yet numbered as national routes
but named by the places they connected
together along a network of the familiar.

We met in a local hotel
the kind found in every town,
famous for its comfort, respectable,
well-known to the commercial traveller
long before he had become a company rep.
Full of mid-week crisis, quotas and commissions.
Arthur Miller kind of people not in turbid America
or in the Waldorf-Astoria, no, just a regular hotel
in the middle of the town
with company reps as isolated as intellectuals.
Dust motes and blue smoke funnelled
by the early spring sunshine above a carpet
which kept the mild hint of stale beer in its weave.

You came, always the generous mentor, to advise
to help and above all to reinforce the need
to keep the word as it was shaped.

To hold the line against the hard demands.
Not to give in. Not to roll over and play dead
for questionable gain. To keep the line
as the line was made.

And then you mentioned the Muse,
a thread of conversation.
Did I feel the intrusion
at the creative moment?
Did I hear the invocation
from the man who sat across the table
as he shaped and honed?
No, these high flown Greek goddesses
did not come between me and him.
There was no ghosting of inspiration,
I heard him breath upon the stairs,
I saw him storm and pale from exhaustion.

But when you set your fancies free
perhaps they will come now to you,
stepping through the cool of morning
across turbid America, Polyhymnia,
Thalia for the laugh and Terpsichore,
light-footed and rhythmic to dance upon
the page.

These other women
these figments of male imaginings,
no, they never came between us.
Perhaps they visit women too,
women who care for rugby,
kill for tickets to Landsdowne Road,
appraise themselves of the difference
between a dithyramb and a loose ruck,

show an interest in politics and play
the currency markets not just the commodities.

But we know our Zeus
that con-man, taking whatever shape or form it took
to have his way and penetrate
the everyday.
And to him a good lay is not just a lyrical poem
intended to be sung.

Her Father Teaches Her About
Real Mountains

for Dervla Murphy

In Lismore
over sixty years ago
the child made
a 'madness of mountains'
pulling and rolling the Plasticine
into flowing ridges and contorted ranges,
into big globular balloons and daft formations.
Spear-sharp, knobbly things,
summits of rounded bumps
twin peaks of gigantic heights and widths:
the child prefiguring the Simiens, anticipating
worlds beyond the beloved Comeraghs
and the jagged edges of the Knockmealdowns.

A landscape in Laos, centuries and kingdoms
from the broad sweep of the adored Blackwater,
there are free-standing eccentric peaks beyond Kasi
and towering above the mud-brown Mekong.

The woman who has pushed passed the giant bamboo –
creaking and squeaking in the wind –
to sleep soundly under a mango tree, who has pushed
passed
the years and the scenes that are known.
That pioneering woman looks out of a tuk-tuk
and sees the reality of her Plasticine mountains
shooting straight up out of the flat land,
and she is back on the kitchen floor,
back in Lismore,
her father telling her, kind and earnest,
in his didactic way:
- Real mountains are not like that.
Peaks don't stand isolated on flat land.

Now that woman knows, and tells us,
that he was wrong.
Real mountains are like that
in Laos.

Literary History

Strange that Miller from Mountrath
should have let Heaney slip
out of the domain of his Dolmen.
Backed a different horse
went with a man much more morose,
you could never imagine him saying
he loved being a Disc Jockey, for Chrissake,
at the solemn end of the spectrum.

I remember Miller too,
the bearded one, the barbarian,
hoi barbari, the clipped prickly kind of beard,
standing on the narrow passage
that is Middle Street, in Galway,
sometime in the 1970s,
having come out of the golden-peacocked curtained
MacLiammoired Taibhdhearc.

Who now knows what play it was which delved
into the depths of perceived dullness.
Who cares, who remembers,
just the outstretched arms of Miller
and the voice taking in all
the boom of a dry-boned and dead past:
Was it for this the wild geese

did whatever they did and fled
was it for this Lord Edward died?

Ah, looking back, always looking back
to Ballylee, to Ballyhoo, to anything back there,
uneasing us in our presentations and in our productions,
mad gone and long gone,
the miserable and the belligerent,
O'Leary and the grave.

The great tradition.
Keeping everything intact, the confused thinking
and the half-thinking, wearing facial hair,
some kind of modish mannerism,
and that it was all *ipso facto* better then.

But the clean-shaven Athenian
comes running down the furrow,
yapping after his father,
running down from Co. Derry,
farming stock, from the hot Gates of Thermopoylae,
running against the destructive forces of time
and obliteration
with a narrative and an ethical form of memory,
with multifarious narrations and nuances.

But Miller from Mountrath,
under the spartan design
of his ancient passage grave
like the Lacodemonian child
left out on the roof to harden off,
fails.

While our Athenian rides out like Arion
on the smooth back of the dolphin
to wash the further shores with song
having mesmerized the greedy sailors.

Travelling West

Wrens flit, cursors on an ash twig.
We wait quietly in the autumn sun.
Middle of nowhere at the world wide web
of blazing rosehips, briars, blackthorns
and the pale bark of ash and birch.
It is somewhere into the West.
There is a dampness in the undergrowth
which will cool the paw of a badger
in the moonlight.
We cannot smell the damp,
we are screened in waiting
for the 13.15 from Westport to Houston to fly by.
The voice activates above our heads:
sorry for the delay, it will shunt past us.
Like hell it will.
There is a suck of air.
Steel rolls and rattles by on steel
and the wheels roar, the sound blinds the eye.
The rosehips sway in the delayed shock.
The light has been sliced into thin slivers
hitting off the unopenable windows of our carriage.

When the eye recovers
there are big blobs of black
plastic sitting on the after-grass,

glinting in the sun.
Malt extract. Molasses.
Sweet morsels for big mouths.
Capsules for giants.

Flight 105

Tower:	Shamrock 105, confirm airborne time and remain clear of Delta 2.
105:	Look ma'am, we've been flying all night, can you do anything for us? We'll have taxied down in three minutes ...
Tower:	I repeat, confirm airborne time and we'll see what we can do.
105:	2.05, ma'am.
Tower:	Alright, move in after Delta 2.
105:	Oh, thank you very much, ma'am.
Tower:	Shamrock 105, continue taxing and following Delta 2.
105:	We've got line-up and we're on track. And we could cope with a clearance if you have it ...
Tower:	105, you are clear for take-off.
105:	Good day to you, ma'am.

I have seen the women's faces, tear-stained,
and the men's faces closed tight as a suitcase.
I have seen them in this place of parting
like some huge funeral parlour, bright and bewildering,
and everyone anxiously waits their turn, doing all
the is necessary and unnecessary
before finally kissing the corpse.

I have seen an unending line of boxes
conveyed slowly into the hold of this aeroplane.
Crystal and china which will glitter on Jackson Heights
or down in South Carolina,
amid animated talk of home and what has formed us.
We know that the delicately-crafted crystal
is carefully packed to withstand
the turbulence of mid-Atlantic.
Yet we ourselves may never be packed well enough
to withstand what awaits us on the further shore.
We can be just as fragile on a snow-filled afternoon
in Jackson Heights, realising that this is a cold climate,
and what we carry with us, behind eyes
which have become streetwise, is as delicate
as a dew-spangled cobweb crafted into a whitethorn bush
at dawn.
Or maybe it is the sand, cut into a series
of lucid and receding ridges, by a slow wave
on Sandymount some summer morning,
and left to burnish in a rising sun.

But the wind comes cutting in from the Atlantic,
we try to climb it and exit into a higher atmosphere,
leaving all those airport faces
with their load of sorrow,
weighing them down like luggage.
Outside there is a bright afternoon
dazzling with recent rain.
Still the wind comes cutting in,
in across the plovers and their complex web-work of
patterns
dashed on the mud of the estuary, ebb tide.

Yesterday, we left footprints on the further shore,
the further eastern coast,
where you must have watched
your own footprint grow bigger with the years.
From shy starts we have moved more confidently
out to where there was a glint of water, way out,
leaving the houses of Sandymount and the Sunday traffic
to diminish in the distance.
Always putting wide stretches of sea and sand
between us and the familiar.

We are not of the static world
that sits and waits and is forever
left behind to paddle the rock-pools
of the predictable.

This time you go alone
among hundreds in the belly
of this machine.
Seated and strapped into position
with all your memories and hopes intact.

Later each of us who has walked
the Sunday beach will take our own lot
out into the unknown
because the wind and the bright afternoon
leading to fields of hawthorn,
and sheep-sweetened mushrooms
can neither encompass nor contain us.

We move out redeeming
the years we have spent

searching for a late and slow blooming wisdom
in a long line of outrageous attempts.

I am in the fields where Runway 24 begins,
you are swinging 'round, lining up,
and on a special radio-receiver,
given to me to give pleasure,
I hear the voices, tower to cockpit,
clearing you for take-off.

Conamara

Mé ar bís roimh aois a cúig dom,
dul siar leo go Leitir Múcú,
is chuig na Doiriú.
Siar amach thar Indreabhán,
thar Shéipéil na Tulaí is Baile na hAbhann,
trí chrosbhóthar Ros an Mhíl,
i dtreo Chasla is i dtreo na Ceathrún Rua.
Locha beaga gorma síor-athraitheacha i ngar dúinn.

I Volkswagon Nick agus Bridie,
an bheirt acu chun tosaigh
ag cogarnaíl leo,
is an gloine gaoithe rompu,
roinnte ina dhá leath
maraon leis an ngloine seang
taobh thiar dínn, mise, Gearóidín is a bábóg
leathan-súileach,
ar an gcúlsuíochán.
An t-inneall Volkswagon do-dhearmadach
ag búiríl is ag glafarnach
díreach ar chúl an tsuíocháin.

Gearóidín is a bábóg níos sine
ná mise.

Mar sin b'iontach an chur amach acu
ar chuile ní.
An chaoi ab fhearr gaineamh-chaisleán
a phleanáil, a dhigeáil agus a thógáil.
Mise is mo bhuicéad ag dragáil an ghainimh cheart chucu.
Gearóidín is a bábóg
ag comhairliú dhom, cá háit, cén sórt go beacht.
An raibh sé ró-uisciúil, mar ghaineamh?
Nó an raibh sé sách uisciúil nó uisciúil go leor?
Seachain do spáid. Cár fhág tú é?
Tiocfaidh an taoide. Seachain an taoide.
Tiocfaidh an smug róin. Iosfaidh sé thú.
Seachain an smug róin. Seachain chuile bloody rud
cois trá.

Ansin, bhí orainn beirt,
is an bhábóg in áit fheiceálach,
tosnú in athuair ar an digeáil i ndáiríre.
Agus tunneleáil mar bhí proper caisleáin ag teastáil uainn.
Móta, bridgeachaí, doirsí archáilte, is túrachaí.
Rinneamar sclábhaíocht air,
Gearóidín chomh pointeáilte sin faoi chuile ní.
Chuireadh sí ceist nó dhó ar an mbábóg
faoi na leaganachaí áirithe,
agus ba chuma cad a tharlódh,
bhí an bhábóg ar aon intinn léi faoi chuile rud.

Bheartaigh an bheirt acu
go mb'fhearr dhomsa dul síos
chun na farraige bige
agus mo bhuicéad a líonadh le huisce,
rith ar ais leis, gan é a shlobarna,
a shlopáil nó a spilleáil ar mo thuras ar ais.
Rinne mé díreach mar a d'iarr sí.

Ach ní raibh braoinín de fágtha sa mhóta
nuair a d'fhill mé le mo bhuicéidín eile.

Bhris na deora orm.
Mé maraithe cheana féin.
Mé strompaithe i dtonnta aeir Chonamara,
is aer na farraige leithne ag ceolán leo
ar bhruach na mara i solas chomh glan leis an gcriostal.
Blas salainn ar mo theanga,
gráinníní beaga gainimh i mo shúile.
Gearóidín is a bábóg ag tabhairt chroí is misnigh dom.
Sos.
Sea, in ainm Dé …
Is seal leis an mbábóg liom fhéin, cineáltas á dhéanamh
orm, mheas sí.
Ach chaith mise an bhábóg as an trucailín,
b'aoibhinn liom an trucailín cheithre roth,
b'fhuath liom an bhábóigín grua-shleamhaineach, marbh-
shúileach, bodhar.

Bhí an-mheas agam
ar mo cholcheathrar is a cuid bréagán.
An-mheas agam ar m'aintín is m'uncail.
Muintir Chonaola a bhí in ann an carr
a choiméad i gcónaí ar an mbóthar oscailte,
scéirdiúil, clochach. Talamh báite, criathrach
is portach ar chuile thaobh …

íseal-ghlór mo mháthar í ag tiomáint abhaile
ó Chonamara, mise taobh léi, ag léamh an bhóthair léi,
sólás éigin i mboladh a cumhra, ionadh orm riamh
go raibh sí in ann tiomáint, go raibh sí in ann tiomáint
leis na high-heels – mé ag clopernáil suas síos an seomra
sna high-heels céanna i ngan fhios di.
- Maróidh mé thusa, dá bhfaighinn tú

i mo good high-heels. Na soilsí ag gearradh
a mbealach dúinn, romhainn amach, an bóthar
ardaithe beagán ón duibheagán ar an dá thaobh.
Dá dtitfimis i gclogar an taobhbhóthair
bheimis inár gcnap maraithe ag briseadh na maidine.
Ach bhí rud eigín i n-íseal-ghlór mo mháthar,
daingean is diongbháilte. Go dtéimid slán,
mar a ndeachaigh sí féin slán, uair amháin,
i gcurrach amuigh lena cara ag iarraidh teacht
ar Leitir Mealláin chun go gcuirfeadh a cara fúithi
sa scoil, an fharraige ag casadh is ag coipeadh
i racht scéine is sceimhle. An currach ag casadh
ar nós chochaillín ... d'inis mo mháthair an scéal dom.
Bhí faitíos mo mháthar fite sa scéal. Bhí faoiseamh
mo mháthar fuaite sa scéal freisin. Dul sa tseans.
Dul i mbaol agus i mbéal an tsaoil nuair is gá.

Carraigeacha móra ag stánadh orainn,
bristeachaí cloiche, fraoch is curaicíní caoinigh
is luachra. Tom is sceach scaipeaithe in áiteachaí,
cnoc is sliabh ar foluain leo taobh thiar.
Tír is tírdhreach nach bhféadfadh bheith níos difriúla
ná an Cheathrú Bhán, m'áit féin,
idir Bhaile Locha Riaich agus Áth an Rí
i gcluimhreacht agus i gcinnteacht na hAchréidhe.

Bhí Conamara cosúil le caisleán Ghearóidín,
ní fearacht an saol agam é.
Dá mbeadh sé ag duine ar bith, is aici a bheadh sé:
bábóg, trucailín bábóige, iad go léir beo friochanta.
Agus samhlaíocht aici is scothóga uirthi mar
shamhlaíocht.
Deirtear go bhfuil gaol eicínt idir mhuintir Uí Chonaola
agus na rónta?
Bhí smut róin is a shúile móra feicithe agam

uair, ar imeall an chaoláire, a cheann ar dhéanamh cheann
bábóige.
Thug mé taitneamh di láithreach, is dá caisleáin
ar a shíodúla, fineáilte, fíor-álainn is a bhí sé.

Cinnte, rachainn ann
chun laethanta saoire a chaitheamh leo
i bhfad ó mo thealaigh féin,
i bhfad amach san aduaineas.
Nach raibh mé fásta suas
i n-aois a cúig.
Nach raibh Joe Mór Ridge
ag feitheamh dom i bfionnuartas an tsiopa,
a bholg mór ar aon dul leis an gcúntar,
dorcha laistigh
i ndiaidh sholas láidir aolghealaithe lasmuigh,
is mámóg mhór mhilseán aige dhom agus guth cineálta:
- Mhaisce, a bhuí le Dia, nach iontach an cailín thú!
- Agus cén chaoi 'bhfuil Annie Joe, do Mhamaí?
- 'Bhfuil mórán gasúr aici? Tú ag cur fút le Bridie.
- Dúil agat san ice-cream? Tuige nach mbeadh.
- Céard sin, a thaisce? Ripple an ea?
- Fan go bhfeicfidh tú. Ó a dheabhaic.
- Cuirfidh Joe Mór ice-cream ripple i gcóir dhuit.
- Maise go deimhin, is maith an té
a bhfuil tú á fhiafraí dhe …

Fós is ionann blas Chonamara agus
cineáltacht Joe Mór is uachtar reoite ripple
feoite idir dhá bhriosca.

Ach b'fhada uaim Joe Mór,
b'fhada uaim chuile shólás
nuair a phreab mé suas sa leaba

i ndorachadas na hoíche is an ghaoth ag búirthíl.
Á mo bhodharú. Na fuinneoga go léir
ag rattleáil is ag bangáil
amhail is dá mbrisfeadh siad uile ina smidiríní.
An teach féin ar crith,
na doirsí ag geonaíl:

    mé sa chuarrach amuigh
    le mo mháthair, cheal máthar.
    Mé ag glaoch uirthi.
    Ise ag dul faoi …

an oíche chomh dubh leis an gcré dhubh
sa gharraí amuigh a nochtaigh muid
níos luaithe chun siúcra, plúr is salann
a fháil dár 'siopa' féin:
Gearóidín ina Joe Mór, mise agus an bhábóg
inár gcustaiméirí. Céard tá uait?

Mé amuigh ar an áiléar is mo philiúr liom,
faoi m'ascaill agam.
Mé sna trithí faitís le heagla,
an ghaoth fós ar thí an teach a leagadh.
Bridie amach chugam, solas léi,
gúna oíche síodúil, Nick ina diaidh.
Smúid na hoíche ar a súile acu.
Iad athraithe san oíche. Síofraí. Síógachaí.
Iad ag labhairt liom amhail is dá mbeadh
pána gloine nó leathán uisce eadrainn.

Gearóidín is a bábóigín
cuachta ina gcodladh.
Cheapfá go rabhadar ann ón tsíoraíocht
cé go raibh an ghaoth isteach sna fuinneoga acu.

Taom cumha orm is sproicht.
An corrgheábh iomarcach.
Giongacht fúm.
Méaracáiní beaga deora,
mé i bhfad amach
ó mo ghnáthóga féin.

Mé i mo chábóg cheart
go béal maidine
go deireadh gaoithe
go héag na stoirme.

Chaith mé an oíche ar aghaidh na tine,
cé gur rugadh is tógadh mo mháthair
i mbroinn shean-choille
b'aduain dom an ghaoth scéirdiúil
i gcoimhdeacht Chonamara.

Connemara

I all excited before I was five years of age,
going west to Leitir Múcú,
towards Doiriú.
Out west past Indreabhán,
by Séipéal na Tulaí and Baile na hAbhann,
through the Ros an Mhíl crossroads,
towards Casla and Ceathrú Rua.
Little ever-changing blue lakes close by us.

In Nick and Bridie's Volkswagon,
the two of them up front
whispering,
and the windscreen in front of them
split in two
just like the narrow window
behind us, me, Geraldine and her doll,
wide-eyed,
on the back seat.
The unforgettable Volkswagen engine
roaring and howling
just behind the seat.

Geraldine and her doll, older than me.
They knew everything about

Everything.
The best way to plan, dig and build
a sand-castle.
Me and my bucket dragging the right sand up to them.
Geraldine and her doll
advising me, what place, what sort exactly.
Was it too wet, as sand?
Or was it really wet or wet enough?
Mind your spade. Where did you leave it?
The tide will come in. Mind the tide.
The jellyfish will come. He will eat you.
Mind the jellyfish. Mind every bloody thing
on the beach.

Then, the two of us had to,
with the doll in a visible place,
start the digging again in earnest.
And tunnelling because we wanted a proper castle.
Moat, bridges, arched doorways and towers.
We slaved at it,
Geraldine so particular about everything.
She asked the doll a question or two
about the particular plans,
and it didn't matter what would happen,
the doll agreed with her about everything.

The two of them decided
it would be better for me to go down
to the shallow water
and fill my bucket,
run back, without slobbering,
slopping or spilling it on the return.
I did just as she asked.
But there wasn't a drop left in the moat
when I got back with my other little bucketful.

I burst into tears.
I was already killed out.
I was wapped with the Connemara air,
and the big sea air singing
on the shore in light as clear as crystal.
The taste of salt on my tongue,
little grains of sand in my eyes.
Geraldine and her doll consoling and cheering me up.
A break.
Yes, for God's sake ...
And time with the doll to myself, as a little treat for me,
she thought.
But I threw the doll out of the pram,
I loved the little four-wheeled pram,
I hated the shiny-faced, deaf, dead-eyed doll.

I had great respect
for my cousin and her toys.
Great respect for my aunt and my uncle,
The Conneelys who were always able
to keep the car on the open, bleak,
stony road. Wet, swampy,
boggy land on every side ...

  quiet voice of my mother driving home
  from Connemara, me beside her,
  reading the road with her
  some comfort in the smell of her perfume,
  always surprised
  that she was able to drive, that she was able to drive
  with the high-heels –
  me clobbering up and down the room
  in the same high heels, unknown to her.
  - I will kill you, if I find you

in my good high-heels. The lights cutting
their way for us, out in front of us, the road
raised a little from the depths on both sides.
If we fall into a swamp on the road side
we will be in a dead heap at day break.
But there was something in the quiet voice of my
mother, firm and definite.
We would come safe,
as she herself came through, once,
out in a currach with her friend trying to get
to Leitir Mealláin so that her friend could start
school, the sea turning and foaming
in a fit of terror and rage. The currach turning over
like a little bauble ... my mother told me the story.
The fear of my mother was woven into the story.
The relief
of my mother was sown into the story too. Chance it.
Risk it and take on life when necessary.

Huge rocks staring at us,
broken bits of stone, heather and tufts of moss
and rushes. A few scattered bushes,
hill and mountain floating behind them.
Countryside and landscape that couldn't be more
different from Carrabane, my own place,
between Loughrea and Athenry,
in the cosiness and certainty of the plain.

Connemara was like Geraldine's castle,
life was not like that for me.
If anyone had it, she had:
a doll, doll's pram, all of them lively
And such an imagination -
They say there is some connection between the Conneelys
and the seals? I had seen the nose and eyes of a seal

once, on the inlet, his head like the head of a doll –
I liked her straight away, and her castle
sleek, smooth, lovely.

Sure, I would go there
to spend holidays with them
far away from my own family,
far out in the otherness.
Wasn't I already grown up
at five years of age.
Wasn't Big Joe Ridge
waiting for me in the coolness of the shop,
his big stomach thrown up on the counter,
dark inside
after the strong lime-white light of outside,
a big fistful of sweets for me and a kind voice:
- Ah sure, thank God, aren't you a great girl!
- And how's Annie Joe, your Mammy?
- Has she a lot of children? You're staying with Bridie.
- Do you like ice-cream? Why wouldn't you.
- What's that, lovey? Ripple is it?
- Wait until you see. Oh, my goodness.
- Big Joe will give you a ripple ice-cream.
- Well surely, you're asking
  the right one for it ...

Still, a taste of Connemara means
Big Joe's kindness and ripple ice-cream
frozen between two wafers.
But Big Joe was far away from me,
All comfort was far away from me
when I jumped up in the bed
in the dark of night and the wind howling.
Deafening me. All the windows
rattling and banging

as if they would all break into little bits.
The house itself shaking,
the doors creaking:

  I was out in the currach
  with my mother, no mother.
  I was calling her.
  She was going under ...

the night as black as the black clay
outside in the garden which we had uncovered
earlier to get sugar, flour and salt
for our 'shop':
Geraldine was Big Joe, me and the doll
were customers. What do you want?

I was out on the landing with my pillow
under my arm.
I was frightened out of my mind,
the wind just about to knock the house.
Bridie came out to me, with a light,
a silk night-dress, Nick after her.
Sleep in their eyes.
They had changed in the night. Ghostly. Changelings.
Talking to me as if there was
a pane of glass or a wide stretch of water between us.

Geraldine and her little doll
tucked up asleep.
You would think they were there since forever
even though the wind was in the window at them.

Attack of homesickness and sadness.
One odd trip too many.

I was restless.
Little thimbles of tears,
I was far away
from my own little things.

I was a real baby
until daybreak
until the end of the wind
until the storm died out.

I spent the night in front of the fire,
even though my mother was born and reared
in the womb of an old wood
it was strange and foreign this bleak wind
in the companionship of Connemara.

translated by Edel Connolly

Broc ar an mBóthar

Tá broc sínte le hais an bhóthair,
cuachta is sínte le hais an bhóthair.
Ciúin, calma, slíoctha
chomh socair sin
gan bogadh.

Broc bocht a d'éalaigh amach
i marbhchiúnas na hoíche,
broc eile léi nó leis,
scata broic i scuaine.
Laige a súl, ag srónaíl leo,
is a lapaí chomh curamach sin
ar theas réidh an bhóthair,
iontach coséadrom, iontach beo.
Is lorg a chos fágtha mar shíntiús
ar dhraoib an taobhbhealaigh.

Líne bhán neamhbhriste ó mhullach go sáil an chréatúir
ar aon dul leis an líne bhán neamhbhriste
i lár an bhóthair.

Cad ba chúis do shiúl?

An mbeidh siad socair sochma inniu sa mbrocach?
Cheal tusa?
Nó an mbeidh do bhris ag briseadh a gcroíthe
chomh maith?
Fosta?

Badger on the Road

A badger is stretched on the side of the road,
crouched and stretched on the side of the road.
Quiet, calm, sleek,
so still
no movement.

A poor badger who crept out
in the dead quiet of night,
another badger with her or him,
a pack of badgers in a line.
Weakness of eye, snuffling along,
their paws so careful
on the even heat of the road,
so lightfooted, so alive.
The trace of its paw is left as a signature
in the mud on the edge of the road.

An unbroken white line from the top to the bottom of the
creature
continuing the unbroken white line
in the middle of the road.

Where were you going?

Will they be all curled up and cosy in the sett today?
Without you?
Or will your loss be breaking their hearts too?
As well?

translated by Edel Connolly

East and West

Yum-Yum lived in Surbiton
she worked for British Telecom
and made long business trips,
on a relatively regular basis,
to Hong Kong.
She was definitely a gourmet
who crept about you telling
of recipes, sauces and how to separate an egg.

She made a perfect Beef Wellington
and though it smacked of empire,
wars, rubber boots, and as British as Britannia,
it tasted very good.
And then her name became a way of saying how good.
Yum-Yum.
She laughed at that or rather giggled
as if there was no way on earth
to insult this woman or say anything racist.
She spoke as if she were British,
she said her Japanese name was too difficult, complicated
for her colleagues and for people in banks,
car rental desks and airports.
She travelled a good deal, why be awkward?

It had some meaning about the shape and sound of water
flowing in springtime across the vibrant green
of saw-toothed leaves just born.
What a mouthful, she thought.
She preferred Yum-Yum, and it must have been
more than off-putting and indeed disarming
in the strategy room of British Telecom,
all starched, polite and proper
to have to address their Marketing Executive
in nursery-speak.
How it must have rung
across the foyer of the Hilton in Hong Kong.
Someone small and quiet and calm,
some little incongruity called Yum-Yum.

She declared that I should have a kimono.
Something pure and perfect that she would get.
She giggled again, joked of daughter-in-laws elect
and mentioned
the comic Irishmen's Mikado.
But how Victorian when an Irishman
could laugh at the Emperor of Japan.
No laughing matter later
with Showa Tenno Hirohito
reigned divine and rapid as a rapier
until the white man reached deep inside
to shape a revenge worse than any known hell.

But this young Japanese woman did
as she had said,
she left a beautiful kimono
with a kind note
on the doorstep in Surbiton.

It was made of exquisite silk
and intricate design.
I wore it and I wore it.
So fine to touch and so delicate.
Then years after, quite by accident,
I forgot it.
And left it in a lovely apartment
where I had slept in New Haven,
Connecticut.

I would never make that trip back
along the road that I took.
The student was graduating, giving up,
moving on, first we *connect,* and then we *cut,*
or so her professor said,
while trying to define Yale.

The student could have put it in the mail,
but it seemed futile, unnecessary, to parcel it
and stand in line
like my relations had done decades before,
either frozen to the bone
or sweltering in post offices to mail
a well-worn but perfect costume
all the way back across the ocean
to my aunt or to my mother.
These women had stayed home,
they knew the fine line and the good cut of stuff,
but Bloomingdales meant nothing at all,
they could only guess at a department store,
a good deal, and a 40% discount sale
for Rosh Hashana.*

*Rosh Hashana: Jewish New Year

So, let us let it go.
Cut the ties to the old anchor,
to place and culture.
Stop hovering between the old and the new,
between the good life and this.
Between the Aran sweater and the crystal glass.
Between the silkworm and the sushi.
But how it resonates.
Now I shall leave the kimono to its own fate,
at Yale, in the late spring, and think of Oahu
and all the hate generated, enough to split the atom,
when with no sound they slipped in
to Pearl Harbour, that Sunday morning ...
And I am in Valhalla, Westchester County,
Gate of Heaven cemetery, with a placid lake,
swans, huge cars which hardly make a sound
as they round the lake and the huge upstanding
marbled mausoleums with Italian family names
harking back to magnificence and Halicarnassus.

Memorial Day. The flutter of stars and stripes
the flooding sunshine, the place is awash
with red and white
criss-crossed above the graves.
My mother's cousin
picks her way in gorgeous clothes
and perfect shoes, to the chair
laid out for her.
And we slip into the Memorial Service
in the blazing sun, we adjust our sunglasses
and think of all those young boys
bagged, brought back,
and buried with full military honours.

This culture is strange to me.

Like eating uncooked fish
and life in Nagasaki.

But I have let it go.
I have left Yum-Yum too
to her adopted empire
and her transnational systems of communication.

We have shared each other's food,
and we have done what we could.

Mary Leary Being Cut Off

Mary Leary drove a big old Ford Mercury.
She cussed and swore constantly:
- that goddamn windshield is smudged.
I paid the guy, top dollar, and look,
the son-of-a-bitch has short-shifted me ...
You can't trust these guys, not anymore,
and believe me, I've seen them all ...

Mary Leary grew up in Kerry,
she knew exactly where, but really,
it didn't matter diddley-squat
whether on the Ring or in Corca Dhuibhne
or not, she was vague fuzzy and
it might be Castlegregory, Castlemaine, Castleisland.
- it, for sure, wasn't the goddamn Blaskets,
got their sorry little butts out of there,
bloody hell, catch me scrimping on that piece of misery.
Her mother was an O'Sullivan,
she herself an O'Connor,
- bet your sweet ass.
I married a Leary, Jim, God be good to him.
Indeed.

She drove that old Ford Mercury hard,
she drove everything hard, right up
the New York Thruway,
Interstate 95, over the Triboro Bridge,
along the thronged Cross Bronx Expressway
hitting the Major Deegan well below Fordham,
crossed the George Washington and pushed
her way down the Pallisades to have a visit
with her old friend from Con Ed, who took
the full package and lived alone in Weehawken,
New Jersey. Her friend Anna, from Con Ed, they worked
at 14th Street for sixty years, was an Hungarian Catholic,
poor dear, no family, not a soul in the world,
lost everything, orphaned, but we look out for her,
sure we do, all us Con Ed girls ... but Gees, why Jersey?
I give her a call. I go visit. We have a cup of coffee.
And then these goddamn Jersey drivers, they
can't drive for shit. They go left on red for Chrissake.
Whoever heard. It does in my head.

- Cut me off! You goddamn son-of-a-bitch.
I'm Mary Leary. You just try it.
Come on spik. Come on nigger,
 in your little piece of imported shit.
Don't you fuck with me, you asshole ...

- What's that? Irish, honey?
You crazy?
Bless your sweet little heart.
Why would anyone speak that goddamn gibberish.
A language for losers. Trust me. Oh yeah,
that's just the kind of thing that'd keep you back in this
country.
Blend in.

She leans into a curve up ahead,
the big solid bench-seat of her old Ford Mercury
is hard and red,
it would push in a face
sitting here behind the wire-haired buzz-sawing broad.
If a truck came careening 'round that curve
a huge gynormous glistening chrome-faced Great Dane,
with twin-exhausts gleaming high above
the cabin, and with an extended nose of steel,
then the world would run her off
the goddamn road.

Riverside Church

Téim thar an eaglais sin
chuile sheachtain nach mór
suas síos an Westside Highway
agus an Henry Hudson Parkway
chuig an George Washington Bridge –
áit ar féidir leat mistéir *of horizontal being* a bhlaiseadh,
gluaisteán leath-dhíonta, an ghrian is an t-aer úr in aon
bhleaist phléisiúir amháin crochta os comhair
dhoimhneacht dhobhar dorcha an Hudson.
Brúnna is árais airgeadgheala Manhattan
á síneadh is á scríobh fhéin
ar fhirimint ghlé-ghorm na hard-spéire.

Rith agus cíoradh na tráchta
cois abhann,
cleas agus cleachtadh na dtiománaithe
spóirt agus dea-ghiúmar
cois abhann
sórt teagmhála idir thú fhéin
agus an carr eile a thagann
ar aon luas leat ó Upstate New York
agus muid go léir ag cúngú chun na cathrach.
Fling deiridh tiomána súl má bhíonn muid
gridlocked sa malltrácht agus i gcoisíocht
an domhain mhóir, beag beann ar na fógraí

WALK agus DON'T WALK
ag síorathrú de ló is d'oíche i gcroílár na cathrach.

Pléascann an ceol latino sa trácht
na mílte dollar caite ar chorais cheolfhuaimeanna
a stracfaidh an fhallaing atá eadrainn,
chuile nóiméad sa chathair seo,
cé go bhfuilimid gualainn le gualainn,
tóin le tóin, cromán le cromán,
ag cuimilt a chéile i ngnáthghluaiseacht an lae
gan cuimilt i ndáiríre
glacaimid, sórt rún-teanga nach féidir linn
an gnáth-chuimilt a sheachaint fad is atá muid
i mbolg an tsaoil.

Ach an Riverside Church,
de gnáth glaotar Rockefeller Church air,
thuas ag 116th agus Riverside,
gan i bhfad ó Grant's Tomb.
Éiríonn sí, mar eaglais, in airde,
gníomhaireacht gan-stadach ina h-ársaí,
is na línte bríomhara
á síneadh fhéin chun na spéire.
Cuireann sí béim ina structúir ar sholas
agus ar spásanna móra faoileoireachta
ag éirí agus ag éirí
os cionn na coitiantachta.
Na túr dúbailte.
Na fuinneoga ildaite ar foluain, go hollmhór
nós cúirtíní Meánaoiseacha
tréansaothraithe.

Éiríonn sí mar a éiríonn, agus mar a d'éirigh,
airgead geal Rockefeller,

mar a phléasc sruth dubh ola Rockefeller
ar fud na tíre seo,
mar a réab sruth dubh ola Rockefeller
go hard na spéire móire Mheiriceá.

The visual aesthetic.
Féin-óltach i bhfoirmiúlachas loighiciúil
na Meánaoiseanna, na Fraince, na hEorpa,
fós ag féachaint siar chun modh is múnlú
a aimsiú dá gcuid airgid
agus glóir do Dhia sna flaithis.

Ach inniu táimid i mbialanna na cathrach
i bhfad níos minicí
ná i n-eaglaisí na cathrach:
agus tá a thuilleadh cháil
ar Oysters Rockefeller -
drop-dead-gorgeous, bácáilte -
ná mar atá ar chúinne bheag a eaglais-se.

Tráthnóna ar bith luath nó mall,
taobh thiar den cheol latino
á chaitheamh i ngach treo i Spanish Harlem;
taobh thiar de na haghaidheanna gorma leath-dhúnta
ag marcaíocht ar an mbus suas Riverside Drive
go dtí 125th agus níos faide ar aghaidh fós, 168th,
Washington Heights.
Aghaidheanna atá fós traochta
ag mindeáil kids na n-uasal
mórthimpeall Central Park,
ag cócaireacht sna joints beaga take-out
i Midtown agus sna cistineacha dhorcha
ar Phark Avenue: great location, honey,
pity about the view –

ag cothú dhea-ghúmair do na white ladies atá
ag peddleáil ar nós an diabhail ar a rothair stadacha
nach dtéann áit ar bith, agus iad as a meabhar le teann
péine.
Ag glanadh Wall Street ó bhun go barr, ag múineadh sna
Public Schools,
ag tiomáint na traeneacha faoi thalamh, ag glanadh tí, ag
ullamhú dí,
is ag seinneadh ceoil sna clubanna beaga chic
i nGreenwich Village ...

taobh thiar den fhothram agus den ghluaiseacht go léir,
briseann guth Martin Luther King trí cheol agus trí chíréib
na sráide.
'Seasca-seacht a labhair sé ó phuilpid eaglais Rockefeller,
Riverside,
frith-chogadh Vietnam:

  'The U.S. Government is the greatest
  purveyor of violence in the world'.

Labhair Mandela ón bpuilpid chéanna sna nochaidí ...

Meabhraíonn gach ní a chéile –
an chaoi ina scríobhann spuaic Rockefeller í féin ar an
spéir.
An chaoi ina aimsíonn an piléar an croí.
An chaoi ina ritheann fós sruth dorcha fola ar an tsráid.

Riverside Church

I pass by that church
almost every week
up and down the Westside Highway
and the Henry Hudson Parkway
to the George Washington Bridge -
a place where you can savour the mystery *of horizontal being,*
an open-top car, the sun and the fresh air in one
blast of pleasure hung over
the deep dark waters of the Hudson.
Glittering Manhattan mansions and apartments
stretching and writing themselves
on the bright blue firmament of the high sky.

The run and flow of traffic
beside the river,
trick and practice of the drivers
fun and good-humour beside the river
a sort of contact between you and the other car that comes
at the same speed from Upstate New York
and all of us narrowing towards the city.
Last fling of the driver before we are
gridlocked in the slow traffic and in the shuffle
of the big world, ignoring the signs
WALK and DON'T WALK
forever changing night and day in the very heart of the
city.

The Latin music explodes in the traffic
thousands of dollars spent on music systems
that will tear the veil that is between us,
every minute in this city,
even though we are shoulder to shoulder,
ass to ass, hip to hip,
touching each other in the usual run of the day
without really touching,
we accept a sort of secret language that we
can't avoid the usual touch while we
are in the throes of life.

But the Riverside Church,
usually called Rockefeller Church,
up at 116th and Riverside,
not far from Grant's Tomb.
It rises, exalted,
restlessly active in its arches
and the vitality of the lines
stretching themselves to the sky.
Light is endemic in its structure
and on big floating spaces
rising and rising
up out of the ordinary.
The twin towers.
The huge stained glass windows floating, immense
like Medieval tapestries
intricately designed.

It rises
like Rockefeller's wealth,
like a gush of Rockefeller's black oil
exploded around this country,
like a gush of Rockefeller's black oil blasted
high in the huge sky of America.

The visual aesthetic.
Self-intoxication with logical formalism
of the Middle Ages, of France, of Europe,
still looking back to find a method and a format
for its wealth
and for the glory of God in heaven.

But today we are in the city restaurants
much more often
than in the city churches:
and Oysters Rockefeller-drop-dead-gorgeous, baked -
is really more famous
than a little corner of his church.

Any evening early or late,
behind the latin music
being thrown in every direction in Spanish Harlem;
behind the half-closed black faces
riding on the bus up Riverside Drive
to 125th and further on again, to 168th,
Washington Heights.
Faces that are so tired
minding the rich kids
around Central Park,
cooking in the little take-out joints
in Midtown and in the dark kitchens
of Park Avenue: great location, honey,
pity about the view -
putting the white ladies in good humour who are
peddling like whores on their stationary bikes
going nowhere, and they out of their tiny minds with
pain.

Cleaning Wall Street from top to bottom, teaching in the
Public Schools,
driving the trains underground, cleaning houses,
preparing drinks,
and playing music in the chic little clubs
in Greenwich Village ...

behind all the noise and movement,
the voice of Martin Luther King breaks through the music
and uproar of the streets.
'Sixty-seven he spoke from the pulpit of Rockefeller
Church, Riverside,
anti Vietnam war:

  'The U.S. government is the greatest
  purveyor of violence in the world'.

Mandela spoke from the same pulpit in the nineties ...

Everything recalls everything else -
the way in which the Rockefeller spire writes itself on the
sky.
The way in which the bullet finds the heart.
The way in which dark blood still flows on the street.

                              translated by Edel Connolly

Fearsaid na Bliana

do Christóir Ó Beaglaoich, dlúthchara liom, nach maireann.

A Christóir, a chroí, faraor.
Tá an bhliain á casadh féin ar a sean-acastóir,
agus mheas mé go dtiocfása slán
i gcasadh na bliana, in am agus in uair.

Feicim tú fós i nga na gréine,
an ghrian neamhghnáthach sin a thaibhsítear dúinn,
Feabhra feoite, Teach na mBád
i Central Park,
is tithe na saibhre á n-ardú féin
trí pheannaireacht shlim an Earraigh.
Na crainn lomnocht
is tusa riamh agus i gcónaí gealgháireach
cé go raibh an tinneas le sonrú i d'aghaidh
agus i ndoiléire do shúl,
ach bhí tú fós fial i do chuid cainte is bhlaiseamar
iarnóin mhíorúilteach Nua Eabhrac le chéile.
Central Park b'ansa leat.
Manhattan cuid ded mhuintearas.
Tú ar do shuaimhneas ar chósta Chiarraí,
áit inár tógadh thú, ach ní coimhthíoch riamh duit

gléghlinniúint Tiffany nó na boutiques beaga
atá scaipthe mar sheoda ar Madison Avenue –
seoda mealltacha na cathrach cé go raibh tusa
cleachtaithe ar ghlinniúint na duirlinge in íseal trá,
ar bhóithre sleamhain-airgid i gCiarraí i ndiaidh ceatha.
Thuig tú saibhreas an tsaoil.

Níl fhios agam an raibh aghaidh an East River dúnta
i léithe na luaidhe.
Níl fhios agam an raibh an ghaoth fheannaideach
á beathú féin ar an Upper East Side
ag 1st agus 93rd?
An raibh an tráthnóna ann
an dúnadh agus an oscailt i gcomhchéim amháin
is an ghloine bhriste dhaite ath-oibrithe ag glinniúint
i gceannaghaidh na sráide faoi dhraíocht na mílte soilse.
An dea-fhocal ag tiománaí bus –
bladhm in aghaidh an duine os ár gcomhair
an Nollaig i gcónaí ann, is tusa, an domhan i do ghlac agat
ó scaipeadh an Earraigh go cnuasach an Fhómhair.

The Year's Axle

for Christopher Begley, a dear friend, who died.

Christopher, sweetheart,
the year is turning itself on it's old axle,
and I thought you would make it
in the turn of the year, in time, in season.

I can still see you in the sunshine,
that unusual sun that ghosts us,
frozen February. Boat House
in Central Park.
The houses of the rich rising
through the thin penmanship of Spring.
The bare trees
and you as always cheerful
even though the sickness could be seen in your face
and in the dark depths of your eyes,
but you were still so giving in your conversation as we
tasted
the miraculous New York evening together.
Central Park you loved best.
Manhattan was a part of you.
You were at ease on the Kerry coast

where you grew up, but the bright sparkle of Tiffany's
was never foreign to you, or the little boutiques
scattered like jewels on Madison Avenue.
Seductive jewels of the city even though you
were used to the sparkle on the pebbled beach at low tide.
Or the sparkle on the silvery roads of Kerry after a
shower.
You understood the richness of life.

I don't know if the face of the East River was shut tight
grey and leaded.
I don't know if the wind was piercing cold
feeding itself on the Upper East Side
at 1st and 93rd?
Was it evening
closing and opening in one fell-swoop,
the recycled broken multi-coloured glass glittering
in the surface of the street under the magic of a thousand
lights.
The friendly word of the bus driver -
a glow on the face of the person opposite -
always Christmas, and you, the world in your hand
from Spring scattering to Autumn gathering.

translated by Edel Connolly

Upper East Side

Going to dinner with Rachel,
in the 80's between Lex and 3rd,
I take the longer route by 79th,
out by the Metropolitan Museum of Art,
well, out by the Met.

Neil Simon walks his dog, or someone's dog,
a small thing, out to smell the air
and mark its territory,
have a pee-pee, make a do-do in
the pachysandras or the pale pink impatiens,
but Neil Simon carries a plastic bag
just in case. No longer *Lost in Yonkers*,
or maybe he still is, but now he is just
an ordinary kind of man, with the stiff
body of someone who leans over a desk all day
plotting the next scene.

Jackie O walks slowly, very slow
in Central Park, she wears the well-known, well-worn
sunglasses, big enough to disappear behind.
Her head is covered, something bright,
but covered nonetheless, she might be
meeting Cardinal Crushing, de Gaulle, a Pope.

She might intend travelling in an open-top
automobile, part of a cavalcade. She leans
on the arm of some man the media say
is a dear friend.

They walk by a grassy knoll
where squirrels flit and cavort. She has become gaunt
from chemotherapy. Soon her children will close up
her delightful apartment. They will have white sheets
and shrouds placed on the delicate French furniture,
then they will sell it. And draw the world to poke and bid
upon the bits and pieces from the halcyon days,
from Camelot.
Golf clubs and cigar humidors,
on and on it goes,
lot number so and so,
her children will turn it all
back into Kennedy money.

On Lexington, Madeline Kahn,
a ghost already from the Mel Brook movies,
wears a light leopard-skin coat and hat
and she is indecisive about a cantaloupe
at a Korean store, where the Korean man
checks the automatic sprinkler system
for his lettuces, come all the way from California.
No shit. And his smiling wife, he never smiles,
out-smarts a lady who kvetches* everyday about
something,
today there is too much green stalky stuff
on the leeks. Cut it off. Make soup, lady.

* kvetch, Yiddish for moan, complain, whine

Or a vegetable stock. The Korean wife smiles
and smiles, she has sold two leeks by weight,
tomorrow that same lady will come again,
poking the aubergine and prodding the zucchini.
I buy some outsized strawberries,
they are as red as red can be,
maybe they too come from the irrigated West Coast,
maybe they come from Israel like the pale endive.
And from the Liquor Store I choose a cool Chardonnay,
straight from the cold chest, it begins to moisten already
in the warm air.

Rachel is a lawyer,
not really into red meat,
likes to cook dinner, sometimes.
She laughs out loud in the cinema,
it is a kind of hoot, people cringe,
you can feel their bodies tightening.
You wait for them to yell out in the dusk,
you wait for some voice to explode
in the narrow mote-filled finger of light:
- Shut up already. For crying out loud.
But they don't, they just don't,
and we all carry on, on edge,
waiting for the next laugh, the next funny scene
and Rachel will hoot out again.
But you and the entire cinema audience
are just a heartbeat ahead
of your embarrassment.

She hates schlock* of any kind.
Loves the opera and Italian food.
If she'd like to be anything it might be Italian,
you know like in an itsey-bitsey daydream for a micro-
second, wouldn't go to the wall on it or anything.
She would hyperventilate, for sure,
spend an afternoon blowing into a brown paper bag,
if she ever had to even consider
living in the country,
nevermind the reverse vertigo she feels
when nothing around her is more than four storeys high.
She could die. Just curl up and die.
Right there and then
if ever she had to leave Manhattan.

She crosses the Park with filial regularity
to see her mother in a Jewish Old Peoples' Home,
her mother barely knows she has come,
on West End Avenue, in the 90's. Rachel
saw Eartha Kitt once in the neighbourhood,
she told her mother about it, and how good
she looked, just there, on the sidewalk with
a *D'Ag Bag* of groceries, Rachel doesn't shop
at D'Aggastino's ... her mother hardly hears anymore,
her life has thinned out
like Novacane wearing off ... her husband, Rachel's
father was a root-canal man,
came from Brooklyn
and has long since passed on.
Her mother is a kind of abstract thing
for whom she pays by standing order.

*schlock, inferior goods, trash

Her mother is a write-off
against taxes when she makes her returns.
Her brother and his pallid wife make a contribution,
they are Zionists now and live near Haifa,
they eat too much aubergine,
Rachel feels, - everyone calls it eggplant, but not she -
too much deadly nightshade and belladonna. Sometimes
she finds them offensive in their thoughts and views,
they argue politics, money, means not ends. They
hate that towel-head, Arafat, always in combat
clothes, they won't give up a stone
of East Jerusalem, not for him,
neither for peace nor Settlement, or any hard-won thing.
But she loves them and their kids, Saul and little Rachel,
named after her. Their lives and stages of their lives
are strewn in photographs, framed and unframed,
throughout her apartment.

She is so giving with her friends, she tells it all,
why have secrets, how much she makes, what stocks
are hot, what stocks are definitely not, she recommends
every thing that has worked well for her: dentist, discount
broker - $35 a transaction, are you crazy, why pay these
guys an arm and a leg.
You'll like Dr Goldstein, yeah, he likes, - *Steen,*
he's good, so he gives a 20% discount on my next
appointment, so it's a win-win.
And she recommends the columns of *The New York
Magazine,* she is not young,
and she has used it to find a man.
Yes, there are blanks, little pools of need, like air-sacs,
empty pockets which bubble up in bad wallpapering.

But they have come,
these well-dressed men from the columns of the magazine
to the Metropolitan Museum.
Or to the delightful Frick, on a spring afternoon,
they have talked
shared likes and dislikes, skirted around difficult things
and kept their balance on a very thin blade on the
Wollmann Rink -
she has skated since forever -
and in chic little places off Madison,
they have dined together.
And sometimes they've just had fun munching
their way through baskets of Buffalo Wings,
all hot-sauced up, and a blue cheese dressing
which lingers on the tongue, close to home.

She's had her fill of the bullshit artists too,
has gotten better at telling them from the real thing.
She has laughed at herself – that special Rachel hoot -
and shared it all with her girlfriends, various nights
for various groups, trying out new venues in the Village,
she has told of the tight-assed schmuck* filling her up
with baloney about boats on Long Island Sound.

It is an eternal hunt to seek out and find
that man to share her bed
and sit opposite her on Sunday in a sweet state
of half-dress,
fingering his favourite section of *The New York Times*
and drizzling maple syrup on his pancakes,
a rush of high-test, heavy-duty coffee freshly ground,

*schmuck, Yiddish, foolish or contemptible person

her eggs,
just as she likes them, easy over, the challah bread
honey-brown crusted with an opening texture
of rich yellow.
Just to have the smell of male shoe-leather
in her nostrils and find his varied array of ties
dangling in her closet.
A man who would rush out to hail a cab –
not a doorman thinking ahead to Thanksgiving –
on 86th when the whole world is frozen stiff,
gridlocked, greyfaced and the slushy mix of salt
snow and grit compounds the sidewalks.
A man to share that cab with her, lean into her
for warmth, set the VCR, confront the water-bugs
who just crawl up out of the drain-holes and sit
like monsters in the sink. A man to like Mendelsohn
and Eric Clapton. To be there, always, a loving face,
a big hug, someone who'll love waffles, cotton tea-towels,
Anita Hill, pecan pie, ass-kicking red hot chilli pepper
sauce, lobsters, not too big,
just with lemon butter, at *Dock's*
and lots and lots of green plants in china pots.

Oh just that he'll be fun,
someone to run to, care for, love to little bits ... just
someone.

At times Rachel feels helpless, exasperated,
with all these would-be partners,
their trial-runs and their dry-runs
and their very few home-runs.
She knows that he must fill the vast reaches of her need
and all the blank spaces, all the exterminated faces:

aunts, uncles, grand-aunts, grand-uncles, mother's
cousins, father's eldest brother ...
Seventeen empty places.
Seventeen blanked-out faces.

Rachel says *kaddish** for them
every time she crosses the lobby of her apartment
building, greets the doorman,
shakes out her umbrella,
the weakened droplets fall, without trace,
onto the marble floor,
as she shakes off the bits of grit and grim attached to her
shoe. And the elevator door shuts to.
And she slips up
through tier after tier of floors and lives. She is devout.
She never does anything as if by rote or unthought out.
The doors of the elevator open back and let her through
out into the space in front of her door,
sometimes she scarcely expects them to, waves of the Red
Sea, and just as she is about to turn her key,
the elevator slaughters the silence
and plunges down the long shaft to lives being lived
below and beneath her.

*Jewish memorial funeral prayer

Beloved

Chuir Giúdach mná ceist orm lá.
Iontach dáiríre fiú.
An raibh Toni Morrison léite agam?
Sea, bhí.
Agus cad é mo mheas?
B'fhiú, arsa mise.

Ba Ghiúdach mná í dom i gcónaí,
cé nár dhúirt mé riamh: -Hi, Giúdach mná.
B'Éireannach mná mise di riamh,
chuile lá is muid ag athrú áite,
ag athrú cainte is smaointe,
gan trácht ar thuairimí.

- Meas tú, an bhfuil na soft-shell crabs tagtha?
- 'Raibh tú i Macy's inné?
Ise ag dul abhaile go luath chun éisteacht le
La Bohème ar fad, ar an hi-fi, ionas go mbeadh
sé ina ceann aici don oíche anocht sa Met ...
ticéad an tséasúir ag Sam.

- Tusa ag dul ann fosta? Cuirfidh mé gloine fíona
in áireamh duit don sos.
- Geobhaidh mé cupán caife dhuit anois, sea, tá's agam,
dubh domsa agus half-'n-half duitse ...
Tóg bog é. Feicfidh mé anocht thú.
- Beirfidh mé *Beloved* liom amárach.
Geobhaidh tú deis blas a fháil ar Toni Morrison.
Rithim phróis faoi leith.
- Bhronnadh an Nobel uirthi:

   Of course I'm a black writer.
   I'm not *just* a black writer.
   The melting pot never worked.
   We ought to be able to accept
   on equal terms everybody
   from the Hasidim to the Rastafarians ...

Thug mé an leabhar di.
Ghabh sí buíochas dhom.
Chuir sí glaoch orm lá, i lár an lae.
Iontach cainteach.
Do mhair an glaoch gutháin uair go leath.
Ise ag cur an chomhrá
sa treo siúd agus sa treo seo.
Ag baint gáirí asam.
Ag baint gáirí as a saol féin.
Bhí sí ag baint taitnimh as *Beloved,*
é beagnach críochnaithe aici.

Gach ní
beagnach
críochnaithe ...

Tháinig *Beloved* ar ais chugam,
bosca Fed-Ex, bán is corcra geal
i láimh an Doorman dom,
nóta faoi iamh,
ag gabháil buíochais
ag gabháil sláin
maidin a socraide.

Beloved

A Jewish woman asked me a question one day.
Quite seriously.
Had I read Toni Morrison?
Yes, I had.
And what did I think?
It was worth it, I said.

She was always a Jewish woman to me,
even though I never said: Hi, Jewish woman.
I was always an Irish woman to her,
every day as we changed places,
exchanged conversation and thoughts,
not to mention opinions.

- Are the soft-shell crabs in yet, do you think?
- Were you in Macy's yesterday?
She, going home early to listen to
La Bohème in full on the hi-fi, so that it would be
in her head for tonight in the Met ...
Sam had season tickets.
- Are you going too? I will pre-order a glass of wine
especially for you for the interval.
- I will get you a cup of coffee now, yes, I know,
black for me and half-'n-half for you ...
Have a good day. I will see you tonight.

- I will bring *Beloved* with me tomorrow.
You will get a chance to savour Toni Morrison.
A particular prose rhythm.
- She won the Nobel Prize:

   Of course I'm a black writer.
   I'm not *just* a black writer.
   The melting pot never worked.
   we ought to be able to accept
   on equal terms everybody
   from the Hadism to the Rastafarians ...

I gave her the book.
She thanked me.
She called me, in the middle of the day.
Really chatty.
The phone call lasted an hour and a half.
She, directing the conversation
this way and that.
Making me laugh.
making fun of her own life.
She was enjoying *Beloved*,
she had almost finished it.

Everything
nearly
finished ...

Beloved came back to me,
a Fed-Ex box, white and bright purple
in the Doorman's hand,
a note enclosed,

saying thanks
saying goodbye
the morning of her funeral.

translated by Edel Connolly

Missing You

for Michael Hartnett

The goldfinch, *An Lasair Choille**,
fires through the memory,
you and Caitlín Maude
in a wondrous combination
of strange imagery and light
out of this world.
You were always out of this world
and in an eternal hurry to be out of it too.
And yet you knew the pain of those
left in the world with no immediate way out,
no easy exit, no quick fix
in the long sentence of mourning.
No getting away from grief.

* Poetic drama in Irish, written by M. Hartnett & C. Maude,
widely produced in the 70s

Such affection of thought
such warmth of will.
Now I follow the vacuum cleaner
along the vectors of a sunlit room,
a late autumn warming, a shaft of sun
and the dust is gathered up, filtered
and sucked into sacks
with the power of 1500 revolutions
whirring through a minute.
It frees the mind
to skimp across the shards of thought and half-thought,
the cluster of years, the voice, the playful and penetrating
brown eyes. The long stretch of road
climbing up out of Newcastle West
to curve and spill down into Teampaill Ghleantáin –
the huddle of cars at the Inn, the necklace of lights,
of houses and hamlets and hillside farms cosy
against the night, hung at points along the Glen,
and all the anger of a language fit to sell pigs in.

And 'all the perversions of the soul'
hung desolate about the highway of the strong,
somewhere in that Munster patchwork of teeming fields
washed down into the rivers which fill the estuary,
as if all the energy was running
out the mouth of the great river
to a squandering and dissipating sea.
Crying the centuries, the old desolations, the cross-
stitched and censoring dispossessions,
crying it into the new century.
A man of sorrow and acquainted with grief.
Lumbering under the weight of the old voices,
the long since dead voices furious with the new order
eating him, pulling the energy out of him
into their dark grip on an obstinate reality.

Ó Bruadair, Ó Rathaille and Padraigín Haicéad
you have pulled this poet into your own perverse
predicament.
Always stuffing it down our necks, the unsweet roar,
the self-pitying cry of the old guard,
furious and ferocious in its fear of change.
It cries to this day,
forgetful of the fact that we have wept
for the hanging gardens, for the old regime,
for the king's head rolling in the dust,
for the blood spilt and drunk by the dark widow
in a market-place, crying the moment out of time,
and into the long dark days of the syllabus,
the must do, the cultural force of our youth,
and we would be shaped by the widow's lament,
a noble O'Connell, a resonant O'Leary
and place our wit against the sparkling voice on the
wireless
telling us of far-off exotica, beehive hair-dos, *stilettos*
and we could see the bright crystals, like soap-flakes
shook through the light to increase the polish of the
floorboards.
The swish and shuffle, the rock and the roll
of the litany of palaces and places of twilit mystery:
The Roseland Moate, The Majestic in Mallow
and the River-rooms in Newcastle West ...
There was a beat, there was an unleashing of the feet
in those well-swept and dusted kitchens, rural but not
desolate, hitching itself to a new state of swinging reality.

For all the chanced times and the meetings in
twenty-five years.
For all the nights that your people put on their
Old Spice and their Brylcreem having washed

the stubborn trace of shit from their hands.
And went down to brightlit warmth of the River-rooms,
to swing and rock the damp fields away,
to cross the line of dream, to hear the Eagles sing,
Hotel California, overcoming the old hatefilled voice
of a dead protesting Ó Rathaille.
To shift, to get lucky, and to get laid –
a culture drained or a culture made?

Finally the Arts Club, Fitzwilliam,
reeking of old and established lives,
of respected artistic pursuit.
You come, late to the event,
straight across the room,
you are already a ghost from another age,
another place,
someone still talks about some part of the event,
the room revolves,
you are slipping before my eyes,
your arms embrace me,
long and hard and tight
and oh so tender.
I am whipped off my feet,
the Eagles sing, in some dream-filled distance
and I hold your frail bones and skin
tight against me
whispering:

Dear Orpheus.

Castlepollard to Finea

I love the road from Castlepollard to Finea.
It twists and weaves and plunges
into dips of narrow possibility.
It has all the features of all the roads of Ireland,
except for the roads on the rim
which wind dangerously in Wicklow,
Clifden and around the Bloody Foreland,
breathless above Kenmare,
hairpinned towards Helvic,
and dangling over Dingle.
They are the exceptions for all of us
who travel deep in the bowl of the country.

The road flows, and the car moves
as if it is on a lifting thermal,
or it is gliding along some invisible
current of age-old karma measured out
in huge stretches of time,
when people made this passage
along a well-defined line linking the lakes.
Young men step back into gateways,
cautious before beckoning on or out
a John Deere or an International,
with front wheels as big and as jagged
as those on the back, all-wheel drive

and power-steering –
but you are about to jump the rise
and twist ever so slightly above him,
there will be no time to stop
for you or for him, he nods,
raises his hand in salutation,
his mouth is slightly open, his eyes stare,
just the merest hint of horror, his gestures,
take a split-second in time and yet
in the thrust and rush of reaction he shoots into
freeze-frame.
But you're already gone
climbing the next incline, resonating in the hedges
alive with birds and flushed
with the lush span of early summer growth.

It is a sizzling sound
as the car tunnels its way through and under
the tender new leaves of broken sunlight
and resounding green.

The road is remembered as being the same
near Ferbane or Borrisikane,
it is the kind of road we will
long for and cordon off in the years
to come,
a sanctuary of real driving,
where you can throw the well-suspended car
with heavy-duty shocks,
into the next deceptive corner
and pull out of it in a lower gear.
There are solid whites which go on and on,
and there are short bursts of broken lines,
just enough to let you take that truck
before the next undulation.

There are signs which tell of wiggles
and subsiding waves, sandpit entrances
forest exits and little pull-in places
where you shall be fined £800 by
the local authority for leaving a trace
of unlawful crap in your wake.
Over the next brow of the next hill
a well-surfaced road reaches
and stretches itself to a foggy vague and indeterminate
point right through the bog.

So fast and furious past clusters of birch,
pale-skinned, bark-shedding birch.
There are vast veins of undisturbed heather
and unexpected cubes of regulated turf
past high banks of piled-up sand and marl,
as if some slow-moving monster had crawled
through this swamp, upturning the earth as it went.

In the straight distance, there is a huge blue truck,
riding the camber, right out, the illusion is
that waves and water are breaking beneath
its axle, and long before you can even read
the legend on its front, you know
that it is one of Sean Quinn's, always heading out from
or home to Cavan, taking and leaving its load
of powdered cement to bind a future shape for those
who dream
in places west and south of Meath.

The truck comes pounding along this road,
filling the view,
we head for each other like impending planets,
vectors of energy, and then, just then,

we both pull in, and pass, yes, it is
Sean Quinn, Sean Quinn, Sean Quinn,
three of them in gleaming convoy
cementing fortunes.

Then like new coins, pure white,
each side of the road, as if spilled
just for the surprise, the fully unexpected,
is a whole covering of bog cotton,
brand new, beautiful and newly sprung in June.

Much further down
past a stand of sitka spruce
the road dives left and leaves the bog.
Then it rises up again
through stonewalls and hedges
of hazel green and banks of tidal, swarming grass
which shows its silver underbelly
as we pass.

Thar Teorainn

A Thomáis Mhic an tSaoir, a chroí,
Uladh is Ultach romham
i ndiaidh fhoilmhe na hIarMhí
is leimhe an Longphoirt.

Nach iontach an mhaise dhuit
i scáth an dúin, ar chiumhais an chaisleáin,
coinneal is béile a chóiriú dhom
i gcompórd is i gcinnteacht
an teacht i dtír
ó scaipeadh na mílte bliain.

Across the Border

Tom McIntyre, dear heart,
Ulster and an Ulsterman in front of me
after the emptiness of Westmeath
and the blandness of Longford.

How nice of you,
in the shade of the fortress, on the edge of the castle,
candle lit and a meal prepared for me
in the comfort and certainty
coming into land
after the scattering of a thousand years.

                                        translated by Edel Connolly

A Glimpse of the Goddess

for Noel Monahan

God, I wish I was a young Guard's wife in Granard
in the 60s, full of promise and hopping with hormones
long before it was fully known what a hormone was, but
these young women knew their power
and how well a young Guard looked
in uniform. A fine thing just come in from the hayfields
of Ballygar and places like it, to sit and swing upon a chair
in the barracks, refreshingly cool on balmy days.

A place with wainscoting, regulation stationery
and a surly sergeant, not a bad auld bollix really,
behind it all, loves the auld flowers, has the place
crawling with them and hanging baskets,
if you're not vexed.
The young Guards pedal slowly out into the damp places
to gather moss for him, soft and interwoven moss,
where he might lay his salvias and brightly-coloured
petunias.

The young Guards sit and swing in the cool, within,
dreaming of noxious weeds and the odd marauding dog.
That's right.
And preserving the scene.
Wondering if hair on the upper lip should be encouraged,
it might seem a biteen silly when hurling with the local
team, the lads might slag the hell out of him –
but still a moustache looks well on Mahony up in
Kilinaleck.

The young Guard's wife is not cramped in or held
high in a tower of stone, no, she glides along a hallway
to a mahogany door, with a fluff of soft pink stuff at her
feet
and a half-concealed negligée of pink chiffon quite full
under the flowing dressing-gown ...
Himself is doing nights and dreams now in the warmth
of their bed of ragwort and fields full of milky thistles,
and go-boys loitering with intent ...
But she comes to the mahogany door tasting of toast and
marmalade.

There is hope and heaven in the very smooth skin
which plunges down from the curve of her neck,
down into places of slight damp and scented nooks.
- It's your milk, ma'am, two bottles.
The young poet stands there with his father's milk in his
hand.
He is in a paroxysm of creative passion which will burst
and rip all innocence right out of him.

The image of the inspiring goddess will stay with him
for the rest of his life,
if now he could only disentangle his knees, his balls,
and the two empty milk bottles
the young Guard's wife passes
to him slowly across
the threshold.

Midwinter Solstice

for Edward Ferncombe and Stephen Galvin

Four hours out of the twenty-four
you both spend here together.
For twenty obstinate hours you are
alone. Confined
with your own daily devices and stratagems
to fill the twenty hours with more than yourself.
Mandelstam filled it with the poetry of her man,
hoping against hope to pull through
and undermine the potentate.
omni potens
the dream state
reaching all the way back to Socrates.
Someone called it *The Republic,*
the things of the people,
and as we sit in this cell, this cave,
I tell you, Edward and Stephen, that
Plato called it something other,
he called it *Concerning Justice.*
And he asked about reality,
he was concerned about shoemakers,
and the City, of course,
that he would ban all poets,
send them to Siberia or Coventry or Portlaoise.

We sit around this very shabby table,
the chairs are stained and caked with stuff.
The butts of fags and ashes and dust.
White styrofoam cups are half-full or half-empty
and scummed with stale cold tea, days old it would seem.
There is a television and perhaps a VCR lurking
behind a big ignorant lock on untreated
medium-density fibreboard, or MDF as it is called at the
DIY.
These doors of MDF are smeared with the finger sweat
of time,
it has magnetized the dark dust onto itself,
like a finger-print apparatus, irrevocable, always before us
as documentary evidence.

There are some kind of blue tiles on the floor,
well they could be creamish, dulled with an eternity
of grunge, it is kind of dark and sticky,
sugary tea has been sloshed upon it
from time to time. And the odd soft drink
for those special occasions, effervescent and loaded with
sugar to ease the moment
and jog the mind with memory of innocence –
first-communions and fizzy drinks, and the stiff visits to
older aunts, grand-aunts,
grand-mothers and auld wans of various descriptions
who plied our youth with sweetness.
If they had no jam for the bare bread and butter,
they turned the sugar-bowl on it, and the white slice of
bread glittered and gleamed
in the half-light of their kitchens
and their kindness in turning our stomachs with so much
sickly sweet.

You both sit and throw your soiled sneakers up on the
table, it is a formica-kind of table.
Then you think, or maybe
see my face and feel some misplaced protest,
you quickly slip the sneakers underneath the table,
and begin to offer me tea or coffee, you take an
assortment of bags
from your pockets, and search for an unused plastic cup.
There is a plastic electric kettle plugged in on a tray on the
floor.
It steams up and sings its rumble of a song, and there is
milk in a half-opened carton,
it doesn't have a poem on it, they must have ceased
putting poems on milk as a marketing ploy and we have
returned to reading
the inconsequential backs of cereal boxes.
Gees, what bright thing came up with poetry for
breakfast!
Breakfast TV is bad enough, but poetry! Perhaps part of
the general penetration
of things, a thoroughly modern regime, an inflated
caricature of modern life.
The Power of the Powerless. You can sit on the subway or
on the DART from Dun Laoghaire
and read New Age moments of noble consciousness
before slashing the seats with a mid-size machete.
Yes, and who plonks the milk-carton bang in the middle
of the breakfast table?
Yeah, right, all those for whom the tea ceremony is loaded
with aesthetic and its history.
All those who can tell their Darjeeling from their Lapsang
Souchong, those who always achieve full infusion and
prefer their Assam strong,
in the normalisation of all things liberal and benevolent.

Ah, for those halcyon days of 'tea and ices and pushing
the moment to its crises'.
And besides is poetry not a pursuit and pleasure of
'cultural capitalists'.
The absolute inverse of the working classes, when they
can get work.
Is poetry now part of the political divide?
The defence of identity and the desire to communicate.
Hartnett thought that 'all poetry was a rebel act',
no doubt those constructing a Platonic Republic
would be of like mind,
though Hartnett wrote about the writing of it, not the
consumption of it.
Is reading poetry a rebel act?
Hardly, unless it extends the shared guilt
of being morally discredited, combined with a need to
violate
all the things which tie us to each other.
Things which bring us into the Havel community
of 'living in truth' opening up a space
of resistance in which antagonisms can articulate
themselves.

Of course, you understand all this special thinking,
you trace the vivid lines of myth and far-reaching
memory.
You talk to me of Joseph Campbell,
that very pleasant man,
who spoke quietly as if out of the mouth
and mind of the earth.
Campbell pulled strands of broken colour
into a prism of recognition.
You both become animated, talking, talking,
through the hours of talk you defy the stubborn and
sullen silence.

You have an understanding of *halcyon*: a bird, a
breathtaking blue and vibrant colour,
a kingfisher, breeding in a nest floating on the wave
at the midwinter solstice and charming the wind
and waves into calm in a clear spread beneath its wing.
'Birds of calm sit brooding on the charmed wave' –
the long line of Milton's tie-in to the creation.
Stephen and Edward, you did not sit
at an oblique angle to the town-clock
on grey mornings of bent heads
in the drone of an old and cranky nun
who had come out of somewhere north of Tuam
in some far-distant youth of hers.
You two did not elbow your way through her accretion
of spite and bitter mouthings after a long and servile life
of polishing silver for the priest's parlour
and kow-towing at office and adorations
to some little bollix with the soup of Maynooth
still thick on his lips. Yes girls, *bollix* like *scissors*,
a good example of the dual number,
where the noun has a plural form only
but comes to be regarded as singular,

there are others in this class: *politics, riches, athletics*
and of course, *trousers.*

Yes, we elbowed our way through her heavy sarcasm,
it hung like jowls, hideous and hurtful, but we found
the magic of Milton in spite of her.
He might have strutted around Cambridge
and swished his academic gown
but he knew the fear of 'a night-foundered skiff'.
He took us out there, out beyond the fear and the heavy
hands telling the time above St John's,
high above our heads

and the undisturbed silence of the Fair Green.
Out beyond the fact that we would never bend the knee
to some collared youth of hurling arrogance and crude
intensity, some red-necked
blustering fellow from Woodford,
Bullaun, Moyaud or Mountbellew.
But this old and narrowed nun had bent the knee
grudgingly
and let the Bishop of Clonfert come to her cell,
once a year,
with big pokey hands and purple socks, for what?
To ransack her drawers and cupboards and little
intimacies, to check her books and beads.

omni potens

We fought and struggled to rise beyond
the grey cell bereft of *billets-doux*,
though this nun could tell, and we knew,
a sweet note, a lovesong, a real poet
and not a bully from Bullaun.
But she had lost her heart
and all was broken bits and malcontent without effect.

  The gumsole creeps up on you, on us,
  whether on the beeswaxed polished floor
  where I have knelt in hindering skirts and folds
  or along the bleak and unforgiving tiles
  where I have slopped out and sloshed
  the foul-smelling bleach in the soured mop.

But lads, friends, sweethearts,
you didn't sit there and take that shit from a broken-
spirited nun from the far-side of Tuam
in the damp days

of a twilit classroom.
No, to hell with that and all the strict routine,
the constant, never-ending, killing tedium.

No, you cursed and kicked and mitched.
Took the track that stays with the canal-water,
right out past the back of your houses,
out to Sallins, to Straffan and Prosperous.
You sat on your ass and flung a stone or two
into the face of the dead canal.
Yes, you did,
in sweaty sneakers and dirt-infested clothes.
You bred your anger and nurtured it.
You scratched your balls and daubed the walls
of the railway track, and smashed some trees and
shattered glass.
You had big feelings for the oppressed,
the doomed and down-at-heel,
you broke into the knacker's yard at Straffan
or was it Sallins,
and set the old death-rowed horses free.

You plundered and smashed the intimacies
of the poor hard-working whores
in their semi-detached places, nustling their neighbours,
for which they took the daily routine, again and again,
twenty hours and four to make a space
where they might dream
until the sun would glaze their bedroom wall with red.
But you cracked the skull of their silence.
You pissed on their well-made bed
and left the track of your intrusive sneaker outlined in
mud.
You whipped the little things and spilled out the entrails
of soft and scented places across the floor.

You violated.
And their right to dream becomes a crime.

Later you would cut a line
of some designer drug, heroin, cocaine.
For whom? For you, or for all the faceless,
ruthless pieces of overdressed slime
who relay your guts and gleaming money
along a track of gore?

When you are crazed, deranged, beyond control,
you know I could smack your face.
What if you let loose abundant thin clear
phlegm and bright red foaming blood
from anyone whom I have loved,
I could tear you limb from limb.
Your blood would coagulate on my hands
and all hope of going home again
would distance itself like the battered and pock-marked
moon.

Well, I think I would.
I think that I could gather up all the outrage of the world
and hurdle it at you.
But no, I'm sure that I would look all hollowed out
and blanked with shock,
as they do look whose cherished ones have been shot
for a wallet,
or punctured in a pool of darkened blood
upon the pavement.
I am sickened by the pain in those pumped out faces.

You confuse me, you two, I am full of affection for you.
But I do not know what to feel – as if to feel I should first
know how.
Who in hell taught me that it is all a progression
to emotional intelligence.
You drain and exasperate me. When they lead you away
and lock you up like some penned animal, my stomach
turns, my heart breaks, just like your balance
when again you will rip through the skin
and throw everything you have gained into spirals of
undoing.

You learn your Spanish but you are no *angelitos*.
Yet your tousled hair spills on its pillow at night,
and someone kissed and prayed to keep you, as they did
the man hidden behind an opaque skin of Perspex,
who stands outside this door with special breathing
apparatus in his suit.
There is a heavy tongue of hard black rubber
on his neck, it hangs down below his helmet.
I have greeted him on my way in, no,
I have greeted them, they are six or eight or ten
men in riot gear, they incline their heads as best they can,
there is only a blank hard surface
where the face should be.
it is a kind of muddied shield, curved and obstinate.
Behind which a man dreams a gift for his child.
Later today he will have changed
and taken his place in a line of shoppers, Christmas time,
he'll know me but I'll have no idea of him.

Edward, Stephen, what is happening in this place?
Something is rising up through our voices
through the tea and this narrow province,
what is happening in this vaulted cell?

I had never noticed the thin grey
panel of glass opposite us,
through it and through the brass keyhole
the light spills in, pours, floods.
The sun is low enough.
Surprisingly.

Or perhaps we on this indicted earth
have tilted and turned
into a blinding alignment of wit.
It is all pulled together in one terrifying stream,
the torrent of rivulets.
This cell, this cave explodes and is awash with light.
The grime and all the dirt disappears.
O Socrates,
we have sat it out, and look, it is a living moment
with all the colours in it.

Coda for Stephen and Edward

And I will think of you between the full green hedgerows
of this evening as I pull up out of Stradbally.
Before I have done I shall touch your faces,
one after one, not in some lusting sense
but with affection.

You are not my sons and I shall not diminish you
in some false and easy pretence of mothering.
You are two young men whom I've met.
You are a warmth in a place of stone.

And hell.
Blow winds and crack your cheeks ...
I cry out of this confusion of steeling myself
to discover how I feel, blindly balancing
your crime, your violation,
on the slim scales of reason.

But nothing releases me out
of what I feel for you.

Na Boird

B'ionadh dúinn riamh móin á meilt acu
agus smúdar móna á tharraingt acu
i gcarráistí beaga bréagánacha
go craos mór an Stáisiúin.

B'ionadh dúinn, lá grianghaofar samhraidh,
lá liathchorcra lár na bliana
cneas an phortaigh briste agus tarraingthe siar acu
is leathnú nach bhfuil insint air
ag síneadh uainn amach
go ciúnas Chluain Mhic Nóis.

B'ionadh dúinn
na carráistí buídhathacha
ag rith ar úrlár mín an phortaigh,
is na milliúin duillí tite á múscailt acu
as suan codlata na gcianta.

Fuinneamh as cuimse, faoi cheilt
i bportach lár na tíre
agus bhíomar ag croílár na cumhachta
ag seoladh solais is fuinnimh
chuig gach cistin is cúinne

chomh fada sin uainn -
go háiteanna bríomhara
go Bailte Móra is cathracha nua-aoiseacha
ina raibh borradh faoi gach ní ...

seachas suaimhneas seanda
na gcrann
is na nduilleog
i ndoimhneacht dhubh Uibh Fhailí.

The Boards

It was always a wonder to us turf being milled by them
and turf-mould being pulled by them
in little toy carriages
to the big throat of the station.

It was a wonder to us, a sunny, windy summer day,
a grey-purple day in the middle of the year
the skin of the bog broken and pulled back by them
and an expanse which cannot be described
stretching out from us
to the silence of Clonmacnoise.

It was a wonder to us
the yellow coloured carriages
running on the smooth surface of the bog,
the millions of little fallen leaves being awoken by them
out of their long, deep sleep.

So much energy, hidden
in midland bogs
and we were at the very heart of it
sending light and energy
to every kitchen and corner

so far away from us -
to lively places
to big towns and modern cities
where everything was pulsing ...

except the old stillness
of the trees
and the leaves
in the black depths of Offaly.

translated by Edel Connolly

The Poet's Woman

You drive, it's his car, it usually is.
You have, of course, given an opinion on the choice,
the mechanical condition of it,
the comfort factor for the long journeys,
the economics of it all,
why you prefer petrol to diesel.
It is a model and make which resonates
at some level in the mind. The kind your father
might have picked. Nothing too ostentatious, solid yes,
but not common and reeking of new money
like those boxy little BMWs, so skittish on ice,
so over-priced, bought by the fleet, yes you read
somewhere that they are such a male kind of car,
all thrust and vibrating exhaust, so much torque
and so many horses packed under that hood.
You can't remember the exact words -
was it a prick car or a car for pricks?
The same article told of the big wide-hipped,
fat-assed, smouldering, purring kind of pussy
cat, with reserves of legendary capacity
and 240 braking-horsepower. A mammy kind of car.
Like mashed potatoes, arrowroot biscuits, tea-cakes
and stew. But the obvious you eschew,
nothing garish, like his output, solid, strong
and inspired by you.

He is not connected to cars, like you are,
he doesn't even drive for Chrissake.
Yet he will know certain historic motoring facts:
Mercedes is Spanish for *mercy*, the German's daughter,
adored and beloved, now synonymous with streamlined
status.
He'll know all about Cadillac and French carriages.
Henry James didn't drive either
Mrs Edith Wharton or was it Ward, drove him here and
yonder.
Not driving is a virtue and your poet will entertain you
on the long hauls with little harmless factoids
about Jackie Stuart freezing off his balls at Le Mans,
in the 24-hour endurance test,
round and round the village,
Monte Carlo and also he'll know of Silverstone
and the theory of streamlining, and minute details
of the internal combustion engine.
He'll even bemoan the fact that there are still
miles and miles of coloured wires, not yet evolved,
under the bonnet or the hood, depending on which
cultural highway you are cruising down,
how to him
the still primitive state of the mechanics is upheld.

He will tell you how the lights extend your eyes,
as he lies back debating if he should read or doze or
dream, or chat through the miles.
While you with a frown of concentration,
hold tight to the steering wheel, the blood has long since
drained from your knuckles
and you know there is that pull,
ever so slight, to the right. You peer ahead
through a film of grease on the windshield or windscreen,
no matter how much you clean, just one bedraggled truck

or ancient belching dream-machine will spew your vision
with oil and muck.
There are things ahead with indeterminate lights or none
at all,
they are crawling around interminable corners
and you are stuck for miles.

It's always winter, isn't it?
With some literary event or reading in Woebegottensville,
where the notion of capital investment
has turned some cowshed into a cultural centre.
Sure they love him still,
he has a fan-belt of deep and rugged appreciation,
it's only the little smart-assed so-and-sos
prancing about his feet in the city, who tell him
that he's past it, that he's old now
and all his best writing was done thirty years ago.
All he can pull now is you.
But you'll keep your youth in his vicinity, in fact,
you'll have found there is no better way,
you'll always look great beside the ageing poet,
and you can tell Elizabeth Arden or whoever tries
to de-wrinkle you to take a hike and keep your money.
Ah, you provide the new lease of life,
the surge and spill of new projects
you make him as happy as a hen in dust
and the smart assed so-and-sos hate your guts.

Fear not, my dear, I know that look in your eye,
the hovering quality in your limbs, in earshot
and yet not quite within the animated circle of chat
and good-humoured remembrances.
Old buddies, faces and friends
who have known him aeons before you had
crossed the Atlantic, been heard of, been born,

and certainly long before he had cocked a leg in your
direction.
Your unovercomeable fear
that they will flock around him,
injure him even in the rush to hear
the great things articulated or just to say
that they stood shoulder to shoulder
with him as he dispensed his wit:
the smiling public man a little coy, a little ridiculous.
But how you hover like a too-hungry hawk
above a winter allotment somewhere near Sallins
or Clondalkin, glimpsed from a hurrying train –
but never anything as demotic, scheduled, confining,
and as public as a train. Are you insane?

But still you hover around the edges of the arts centre,
an ever-watching lover, because there are those
bright young things
with a thesis or two and even more energy than you,
ready to give it all
and drive the distance.
And there are the little boys, you know the type,
they come laden with sheaves of manuscript
manicured and tabulated, they reek of temperament,
make all the right moves, they want to bed their Socrates,
ply him with gifts, give themselves like Alcibiades,
not to worry honey, he's been fielding them for years,
at bottom, it's generally a case of aesthetic disposition,
cant, rant and fuck-all talent.

But the older, riper ones, watch them,
blue-stockinged or stockingless, hard to tell,
they have long foregone the blessings
of a good knickers.
Remember Robert Lowell

telling of his first kiss, girls sailing and having fun
in North Haven, making great discoveries
in the blue frontiers of the bay ...
These older ones anchor him to the past,
safe and familiar, they have matured
into a Lisadell version of the beautiful.
They are mindful, subtle and dab hands with the gel –
the old hormone-replacement thing,
no aridity now, no vaginal desiccation,
but a prolonged tír-na-nógness,
a definite rise to the occasion.
A blonde-headed Niamh on horse-back,
hell-bent on luring the love-consumed one
into a mad rush of youth.
That kind of blooming intelligence is lethal, my dear.
You're never any match for it when the legal wife
gives over crying in her soup while lunching
at the National Gallery, of course she thinks
you're a clever little bitch, but she only tells that
to her diary and the ladies who lunch, and they agree,
but they don't give a shit for your research
and as to the biography you'll never get access.
They remind themselves that Clinton fell
for that endearing little slut who could give such head
and not the Prioress type, Secretary Albright.
Just a little time, and a mature stratagem.

You see, you have no ring, and there are the naked
moments of being in places where people hold
your hand too long, ooze their sorrow onto you,
glad, sad and mad too that the good screw
is no longer you.
They need him for the Christmas gig, the Festival thing,
now you're not worth a pin.
Oh they love you,
they feel for you,

but they'll still ask him,
they'll rattle up a few tired flowers
for you in crinkled cellophane.
They'll balls up the beds,
though you'll have driven, if you want the ensuite
you'll have to take the twin, a couple
of monastic singles with the bedclothes
battened down, otherwise it's a mile
to the bathroom and sure as hell
that randy old hoor from Revenue
will be lurking in some nook or cranny
now that he's had a poem in *Poetry Ireland Review*
he's bought himself a time-share
in every shagging shindig from here to Killaloe.

In fact you may find yourself offering to pay
the extra supplement just to be included in,
but soon you'll be a has-been
a classic hit of the 90s
a Huston outfoxed by Nicholson,
a limping lightweight
a poor forgotten pinfeathered mother hen.

Visiting in Cavan

for Tom McIntyre

Thomas McIntyre, kinsman of Ciarán –
who in the quiet of Clonmacnoise
must have seen the wall of green and vibrant
trees break damp and delicate leaves
along the slow and far-reaching Shannon.

You too, son of the free and the craftsman,
sing on that line of Sheelin where earth
meets sky in the water's face and holds
eternity for a split and sparkling second.

You've collected brosna and kindled
the warmth of your mother's word
beyond Virginia, Achadh an Lúir,
all is intact and incorruptible.

To love, to monk it or go mad
along the clear green tracks the ice has made
down to the water's edge you dream the fine line,
give it life, coaxing it out of the dark.

Na hUachaisí is na hÁfachaí

do Chathal Ó Searcaigh le cion nach beag

Muid beirt céim ar chéim linn
ar shráideanna Chorcaí, cois Laoi,
éalaithe uathu, sos beag san oíche,
is an aimsir ag piastáil chun báistí.
Taise na habhann is na bhfarraigí
i gcartadh an aeir, ach ba bheag orainn é.

Sos beag ón gcaint laistigh agus blas na tequila sunrises.
Na titimeacha smaointe ag casadh i gcomhluadar
fhoireann Shlógadh.
Rinne sí an-oíche airneáin
ach d'éalaíomar uathu ar feadh seal.

Lasmuigh, thosaigh an oíche ag méadú is ag forlíonadh
eadrainn.
Draíocht bheag dhiamhair áirithe
sna súilíní machnaimh á roinnt againn.
Ní raibh ann ach go bhfeicfeá
d'aghaidh is do chruth dea-chumtha
fad is a bhí an solas sráide á shuaitheadh féin
anonn is anall thar phíchairt na gealaí.

An cine dar díobh thú, ag eisileadh ó do chliabhrach.
Leoithne ón anallód, ag cothú suaimhnis duit.
An cine dar díobh mé, beagáinín fós sa chlapsholas,
an uair úd. Tusa riamh ar leac deimhne.
Mise in amanna liongánach agus leath-chosach
sna lonnaigh laga in íochtar dí-thrá.

Do chasamar beirt ár n-uillinneacha
ar uchtbhalla na habhann.
Bhí na healaí ina dtaibhsí fúinn,
is an taoide ag rith is ag coipeadh
i gcoirí guairneáin ag éalú uainn.

Cathair aduain.

D'fhiafraigh tú díom gan fiafraí,
is ní bhfuair tú faisnéis.

D'imigh an nóiméad tharainn
i gCorcaigh cois Laoi na Sreabh.
Go bhféacha Dia orainn!
Rudaí óga geala!

Tamall den bhóthar a shiúl leat,
tamall den bhóthar a shiúl liom,
is tuilleadh thar ár gcion ar bord,
nach aoibhinn an mhaise dúinn.

Chuamar amach i gcoinne na tuisceana,
chun teacht uirthi mar thuiscint,
mar a théimid fós is fosta leath na gcuarta.
Tá thoir is thiar cuartaithe is siúlta againn,
thar bhreaclachaí is broclachaí an tsaoil.
Agus na háiteanna atá aimsithe againn
tá siad anois ag soilsiú go glé
is ár súile i dtaithí orthu cheana féin

Is aoibhinn linn an siolla gaoithe,
an t-aer chomh bog le tuáille,
is sna blianta romhainn amach
guím go bhfaighimid i gcónaí friotal friseáilte
do na cíocha nua-bhioraithe
is an caoineas beag i gcuar an bhoilg.
Is go raibh solas na gréine ag neadú
is ag súgradh i bhfionnfholt do thaisce.

Nithe ní ba ghlé
ná glinniúint na mílte mirlíní nua.

Is go raibh an focal i gcónaí beo ar do theanga.

The Whys and The Wherefores

for Cathal Ó Searcaigh with great affection

The two of us walking step by step together
on the streets of Cork, by the Lee,
escaped from them, a little break in the night,
the weather changing gradually to rain.
Dampness of the river and moisture of the sea
in the gathering air, but it doesn't bother us.

A little break from the conversation inside and the taste of
the tequila sunrises.
The run of ideas twisting in the company
of the Slogadh team.
It was a great social evening
but we escaped from it for a while.

Outside the night started growing and filling
between us.
A small particular deep magic
in the stream of thoughts being shared between us.
All that could be seen was
your face and your well-shaped body

while the light of the street was swinging itself
back and forth over the pie-chart of the moon.

The people to whom you belong, enriching you.
Light breeze from long ago, putting you at ease.
The people to whom I belong, still a little in the twilight,
at that time. You always surefooted.
I, sometimes unsteady with one foot
in the soft rippling waves of low tide.
The two of us threw our elbows
on the parapet of the river.
The swans were ghosts beneath us,
the tide running and swirling
in the whirlpools slipping away from us.

Unfamiliar city.

You asked me without asking,
you were given no clue.

The moment passed
in Cork beside the flowing Lee.
God love us!
Bright young things!

Walked a bit of the road with you,
walked a bit of the road with me,
a little intoxicated,
wasn't it wonderful for us.

We went out searching for wisdom,
to find understanding,
as we still go more often than not.
East and West we have visited and walked,
over the stony ground of life.
And the places we have found
are now shining brightly,
our eyes have got used to them already.

We love the hint of a breeze,
the air as soft as a towel,
and in the years to come
I hope that we will always find fresh phrases
for the newly pointed breasts
and the little softness in the curve of the stomach.
And may the sunlight nestle
and play in the fair hair of your sweetheart.

Things brighter than
the sparkling of a thousand new marbles.

And that the word may always be alive on your tongue.

translated by Edel Connolly

The Writer's Wife

after John Banville, reviewing Vera Naborov's biography
in *The Irish Times*, 1999

Who would be a writer's wife?
Condemned to a life of helping,
nursing, mothering and elbowing
the muse and her sisters out of the bed.
Who would have the life?

  - Oh, I spoke to you on the phone,
  that's right, it's Mary, isn't it?
  You do all the typing, I suppose,
  lucky man, he never said ...
  Oh, your name is Anne, and with an 'e'!
  Gee, I could have bet my bottom dollar
  it was Marie, must be someone else ...
  and are you familiar with that poem?

There is so much surprise in the voice
that you would be familiar with anything
least of all a poem. You ought to be
some ninkampoo like Nora, who never read

all that auld rubbish, Jim said, Jim always said …
And in the lean years
you scrimped and saved and bravefaced it.
Beans and brown rice made protein,
you rattled up new outfits from old clothes.
You borrowed from your mother, even,
who told you so, how it would come to this,
and still you married that dosser, couldn't keep a job.
Writing is it?
Who the hell will read it anyway?
It'll always be a poor day.

The few friends you have pity you,
you've been nowhere, don't go anywhere,
you've lost the urge to shop,
you'd never play golf, never need a make-over,
you're fat, still fertile, they feel, a lot of flab,
unwanted hair and in need of a totally new wardrobe.

Of course he is on full inspiration in high summer,
must stay in bed all day, not go away, remain
shuttered up in sweltering heat, won't eat salad,
it's not an inspiring kind of food.
God, have you kept those slugs off the lettuce
and pigeons too
who sneak in on an early wing and munch away,
big globs of your Cos and Boston heads,
quiet and destructive buggers who shove out their chests
and chew.

Then he's up all night.
Pacing back and forth.
Flushing the toilet and whapping up the seat,
sounds which carry and hit off the plasterboard,

reverberate in the trapped air and space
of the studded parting walls.

It's his best novel yet.
A masterpiece.
An ideal filmscript.
A sure thing. A best-seller.
A knock-out, a killer, a dead cert ...
Yet you keep the faith.
Guard the flame.
Comfort him when he's depressed –
which is always and ongoing.
He's depressed before he writes it,
afraid he cannot start it.
He's depressed while he is writing it,
afraid he cannot finish it.
He's depressed when it is written
afraid he'll never write another word again.

For launches, publications, parties,
first-nights and presentations,
your name is 'Guest',
not even Mary or Anne,
and if it's Irish
then you're a grammatical tag-on:
agus a bhean.

And when affluence comes along a well-tried trajectory,
and cheques roll in from unexpected places,
when you both feel it is not a fee
but prepayment for twenty books, for a lifetime,
then it's 'booze and birds',
bonhomie
camaraderie

and lavish gifts for those to whom
he feels some misplaced indebtedness.
Your mother is still owed,
- that auld bag, he says, never believed in me.
Now you protect the great man
from the screw-balls and the fans.
You arrange private little get-aways
with people who own houses and islands,
of course they're philistines, he was right,
but you undo, as best you can, the digs and cuts,
the downright insults
by blaming the age-old artistic temperament.

You stand for hours, having been pushed aside
at some reception, ignored and overlooked
like a piece of regular junk.
You are sidelined in the stampede
once they've spotted him,
until some understanding matron-type,
who is there herself by default, out on a bit of a limb,
tracks you down and plies you with banalities,
sticks by you, ushers you to your seat, remains there too,
right up against you, just in case, she's got a thin
and ugly face, they always do, and just by doing this
she feels she has struck up some kind of undying
friendship
to which she will refer at dinner parties,
and tell how seeing you so neglected
she understood
as only a woman could ...

Through the throngs you spot a face, a friend indeed,
from years ago, who smiles and signs to you to slip on out
to some local pub, let all this go, for a chat, a bit of normal
intercourse,

a gin and tonic,
where you can be yourself and swear, laugh and not give
a cobbler's
for all their high art
and esoteric crap.

But God, if you should outlive him
and all the hectic comings and goings,
forget the mourning,
they will resent you for just being alive.
Publishers will call you 'she'
and hate every single moment of the seventy years
after his death when they have to ask you,
little old you, permission for every word,
when they must credit, acknowledge you
and worst of all: pay you too.

All researchers will hate you to the core.
They will plot among themselves
and compare the bits and pieces
they have squeezed and inveigled out of you.
They will double-cross each other, pretend no thesis,
they will survive to deliver yet another paper
proving the long-held belief that you are hiding
something.

Why else would you be a writer's wife?

Turas na hOíche

do Michael Hartnett nach maireann

Glaonn an *muezzin* ó bharr an *minaret*
sa dorchadas. Táimid inár suí ar bhalcóin,
crochta os cionn an chuain.
Tá na báid ceangailte le chéile
i mbráisléad soilse thíos fúinn.
Tá fhios againn freisin
go bhfuil áirsí ársa gearrtha sa chloch fúinn,
gearrtha in aghaidh na haille, is ansin
san anallód a bhíodh na tógálaithe long
ag cur allais sa chlapsholas
ag iarraidh slat éigin a chur
idir iad fhéin agus an faitíos.
An longbhriseadh -
i mbéal farraige
i mbac carraige
i ndeireadh dóchais nuair a chasann
an Líonán isteach orainn.

Muid ar bhruas aille
i séimhe na moch-oíche,
glaonn an *muezzin* ag moladh *Allah*,

an glao chun na bpaidreacha.
Níl aon *qiblah* agam, an compás úd
a aimseoidh Mecca is an *Ka'bah* dom.
Spréann guth is cantaireacht an *muezzin*
amach thar réimsí na Meánmhara
atá chomh gorm le hubh na spideoige broinndeirge.
Fiú san oíche, is geal, solasta fós an chuimhne,
an dath sa tsúil ó ghlé-ghrian an lae.

Sileann guth an *muezzin*
ar shruthanna gile na cuimhne.
An Lasair Choille - tú fhéin is Caitlín Maude,
file eile ar bís chun teacht i gcomhluadar a sinsear,
amhail is dá mba ar strae anseo dhaoibh beirt.
Ag iarraidh briseadh éigin a aimsiú san fhallaing,
sa Dreamtime, san aghaidh fidil, an bealach isteach
is an bealach amach trí gheata geal na síoraíochta
dod mhuintir fhéin a d'éag roimh bhás do Chríost.

Sileann guth an *muezzin*, éiríonn an ghealach dheirceach
ar chósta na dTurcach, ar sheanbhealaí an tsaoil
idir an Domhan Thoir agus an Domhan Thiar.

Na cosáin trádála, is na camaill
ag coiscéimíocht go cúramach faoina lastaí cumhra,
ó ósta go hósta go dothuirsithe.
An ghrian scólta i bhfad uainn
i dTeampall Gleanntáin ...
ach nach tusa a bhíodh cleachta
ar an scóladh croí is anama.

Tusa, níor mhaith leatsa mo bhris,
bhí do ghuth is do dhea-ghuí

mar ghlao glinn an *muezzin*
san oíche agam.
Thuig tusa na rithimí is na roilleacháin
faoi thoinn, thuig tusa tarraingt na toinne
i gcasadh na gealaí.
Thuig tusa na híomhánna léirscríofa
i gcipín an gheimhridh faoi chos bhideach
an dreoilín.

Músclaíonn an *muezzin* an slua san Arts Club,
i bhFitzwilliam, an uair dheiridh dhúinn,
cé nach raibh fhios againn, ní bhíonn fhios.
Ní bhíonn ach seal ar cíos.
Ba chuma faoin gcaint, ba chuma faoin óráidíocht,
tháinig tusa díreach chugam go tóin an tseomra
ina raibh sprid an tseandreama ón tsean-am ar foluain leo
ina dtábhacht fhéin agus muidne, éigseoirí an lae inniu
ag iarraidh an nóiméad a bhlaiseadh, casadh eile
i saol liteartha na haimsire seo.

Tháinig tusa chugam, do ghéaga spréite,
barróg chiúin, thostach, barróg fhada insínte.
Ní raibh ionat a chroí, ach cnámharlach,
fós te teolaí, ach creatlach i mo lámha agam
ar critheagla ar mo chliabhrach.
Nach rabhamar go léir inár n-éalaithigh ón mbás,
agus nach raibh an bás féin ag teannadh isteach linn.
Bhí sé ag glaoch ort le fada, a chroí.

Éalaíonn bád amach uainn ar aghaidh na mara fúinn,
iontach seoigh, iontach ciúin.
Lasta lonrach ag sleamhnú uainn amach
go mbrisfidh glór an *muezzin*
isteach ar an mbrionglóid agus beidh tusa

i gcomhluadar na mórfhilí a chum is a chan
ar shleasa bána na Mumhan,
roimh scéal geal *Allah*,
roimh bhás do Chríost
agus rós ar do ghualainn agat.

Night Journey

for Michael Hartnett, who died

The *muezzin* calls from the top of the *minaret*
in the dark. We are sitting on a balcony
overhanging the harbour.
The boats are tied together
in a bracelet of light below us.
We also know
that there are ancient arches cut in the rock beneath us,
cut into the face of the cliff, and there
long ago ship builders
sweated in the twilight,
trying to put some kind of a plank
between themselves and fear.
The shipwreck –
in the mouth of the sea
in the undoing rock
in the last hope when the Lagoon
spills in on top of us.

Us, on the edge of the cliff
in the mild early night,
the *muezzin* calls praising *Allah,*

the call to prayer.
I don't have any *qiblah*, that special compass
which will lead me to Mecca and the *Ka'bah*.
The voice and chanting of the *muezzin* spreads
out over the expanse of the Mediterranean
as blue as the redbreasted robin's egg.
Even at night, the memory is still bright and lit,
the eye holds the colour of the sun-lit day.

The voice of the *muezzin* spills
along the bright streams of memory.
The Gold-Finch – yourself and Caitlín Maude,
another poet anxious to join her ancestors,
as if the two of you were astray here.
Trying to find some opening in the veil,
in Dreamtime, in the mask, the way in
and the way out through the bright gate of eternity
to your own people who died before the death of Christ.

The voice of the *muezzin* spills over, the crescent moon
rises on the Turkish coast,
on the old routes of life
between the Orient and the Occident.

The trade routes, and the camels
stepping carefully under their fragrant loads,
from inn to inn, tireless.
The scalding sun far away from us
in Templeglentan ...
but you were used
to the heart-scald.

You, you were sorry for my trouble,
your voice and good wishes
were like a clear call of the *muezzin*
in the night to me.
You understood the runs and the rills
underwater, you understood the pull of the waves
in the turning of the moon.
You understood the clearly written images
in the twig of winter under the tiny foot
of the wren.

The *muezzin* awakens the crowd in the Arts Club,
in Fitzwilliam, the last time for us,
even though we didn't know, we never know.
We only have a time on lease.
Conversations didn't matter, speeches didn't matter,
you came straight over to me at the back of the room
where the spirit of the old crowd from the old times
floated
in their own importance and we, writers of today
trying to taste the moment, another turn
in the literary life of our time.

You came over to me, your arms outstretched,
quiet embrace, silent, long extended embrace.
You were only a skeleton, dear heart,
still warm and tender, but a skeleton in my arms
trembling on my chest.
Weren't we all escapees from death
and wasn't death itself tightening itself in on us.
It was calling you for a long time, dear heart.

A boat moves away from us out onto the seas,
very charming, very still.

A shimmering load slipping away from us
the voice of the *muezzin* will break
in upon the dream and you will be
in the company of the great poets who wrote and sang
on the white slopes of Munster,
before the bright story of *Allah*,
before the death of Christ
with a rose on your shoulder.

translated by Edel Connolly